SEAFARING AND CIVILIZATION

Philip de Souza was born in Usk, South Wales, in 1964. He studied
History and Classics at Royal Holloway College, University of London.
He is a Senior Lecturer in the Department of Historical, Social and
Cultural Studies at St Mary's College, Strawberry Hill. He is a member
of the Nautical Archaeology Society and a Fellow of the Royal
Historical Society. His recent publications include *Piracy in the Graeco-
Roman World* (Cambridge, 1999). He lives in Surrey with his wife,
Debra, who is also a historian.

PHILIP DE SOUZA

SEAFARING AND CIVILIZATION

MARITIME PERSPECTIVES ON WORLD HISTORY

P

PROFILE BOOKS

First published in Great Britain in 2001 by
Profile Books Ltd
58A Hatton Garden
London EC1N 8LX
www.profilebooks.co.uk

This paperback edition first published in 2002

10 9 8 7 6 5 4 3 2 1

Typeset in Minion by MacGuru
info@macguru.org.uk
Printed and bound in Great Britain by
Bookmarque Ltd, Croydon, Surrey

A CIP catalogue record for this book is available from the British Library.

ISBN 1 86197 323 3

Cover illustration This is taken from a panel of the Perugia Triptych, painted by Fra Angelico (Guido di Piero, *c.*1400–1455) for the chapel of St Nicholas in the church of San Domenico, Perugia, in 1437. It shows two posthumous miracles of St Nicholas, patron saint of sailors and merchants. On the right, he saves mariners who pray to him when their ship is caught in a storm. To the left, a famine is averted when grain is delivered to the saint's home city of Myra in Lycia, thanks to his appearance before an envoy of the Roman emperor

CONTENTS

PREFACE

This book has been written to accompany the 70th Anglo-American Conference of Historians at the Institute of Historical Research, University of London, the theme of which is 'The Sea'. Thanks are due to the Director, Professor David Cannadine, for having the confidence to invite me to write it, and to his predecessor, Professor Patrick O'Brien, for inviting me to participate in his stimulating seminars on Global History at the Institute of Historical Research, sponsored by the Renaissance Trust, from which I learned a great deal.

A work of this kind necessarily relies upon the publications of many distinguished scholars, who are not responsible for any errors I may have made in my use of their works. I have concentrated to some extent on the ancient, medieval and early modern history of the civilizations of Europe and the Mediterranean, but this is partly due to the nature of the arguments put forward and also because it is where my own expertise is strongest.

I would like to thank Dr Ted Kaizer and Ms Leonora Miles who took over some of my undergraduate teaching commitments, partly financed by a grant from the Research Support Fund at St Mary's College, Strawberry Hill. Several academic colleagues provided valuable advice and assistance during the writing, especially Dr Michael Partridge and Dr David Evans at St Mary's, and Professor Frances Berdan at CSU San Bernardino. The book could not have been researched and written without the libraries of the University of London, the Institute of Historical Research, the Warburg Institute, the Institute of Commonwealth Studies, Royal Holloway, the Ashmolean Museum and St Mary's College.

Many people have helped in the preparation of the finished volume, but special thanks go to Josine Meijer, who sorted out the illustrations; everyone at Profile Books, especially Peter Carson, a very patient editor, Penny Daniel and Bela Cunha, the copy editor.

As always, I owe the greatest debt to my wonderful wife, Debra, whose support, advice and encouragement have been invaluable.

Finally, I dedicate this book with love and thanks to my parents, Collin and Maureen, who often took me to the seaside as a child and have supported all my academic efforts with great encouragement and affection.

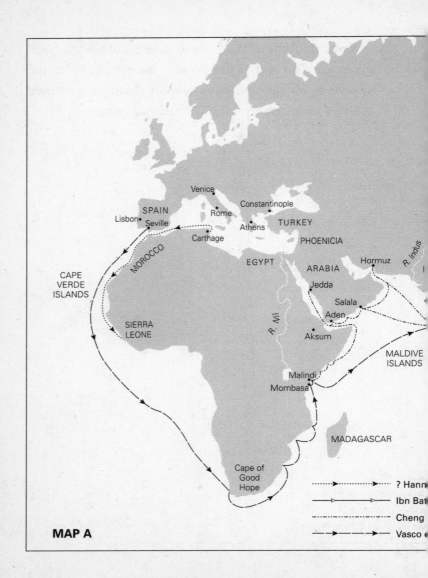

MAP A

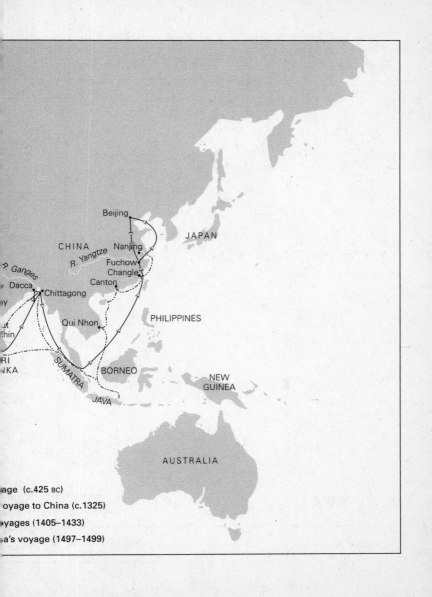

Beijing

CHINA

R. Yangtze

Nanjing

R. Ganges

Dacca

Chittagong

Fuchow
Changle

Canton

JAPAN

Qui Nhon

PHILIPPINES

SUMATRA

BORNEO

NEW
GUINEA

JAVA

AUSTRALIA

...age (c.425 BC)

...oyage to China (c.1325)

...yages (1405–1433)

...a's voyage (1497–1499)

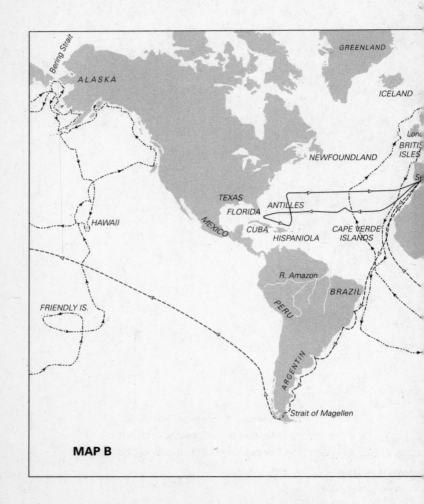

MAP B

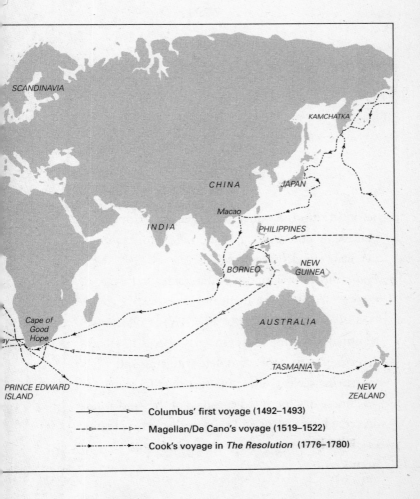

SCANDINAVIA

KAMCHATKA

CHINA

JAPAN

Macao

INDIA

PHILIPPINES

BORNEO

NEW
GUINEA

Cape of
Good
Hope

AUSTRALIA

TASMANIA

PRINCE EDWARD
ISLAND

NEW
ZEALAND

——▷——▷—— Columbus' first voyage (1492–1493)

--▷-----▷-- Magellan/De Cano's voyage (1519–1522)

-·-▶-·-·-▶-·- Cook's voyage in *The Resolution* (1776–1780)

LIST OF ILLUSTRATIONS

While every effort has been made to trace copyright
holders for illustrations featured in this book, the
publishers will be glad to make proper acknowledgements
in future editions in the event that any regrettable
omissions have occurred at the time of going to press.

INTRODUCTION

THE CHALLENGE
OF THE SEA

*Many and terrible are the wonders to be found, and none more so
than mankind, the most terrible wonder. Traversing the foaming
sea, driving forward through storms and gales as waves surge all
around, he struggles to hold a steady course …*

*… Man is master, his genius is beyond all compass, beyond all
imagining are the skills at his disposal – he strives onwards, at one
moment to disaster, in the next towards triumph …*

(Sophocles, *Antigone*, 331–5; 376–81)

These verses, taken from the tragic play *Antigone*, written in
the middle of the fifth century BC by the Athenian poet
Sophocles, invoke both the benefits and the dangers inherent in the challenge of seafaring. They are also a metaphor

for the double-edged sword of human ingenuity and genius – the capacity to create and to destroy. Throughout the history of the world the sea has offered a powerful medium for the development and expansion of human societies and it has been a conduit for the dissemination of both positive and negative aspects of civilization.

This study explores selected themes in the development of human civilizations, as seen from a maritime perspective. It does not aim to provide comprehensive coverage of world history in chronological or geographical terms. Rather it seeks to show some of the ways in which seafaring has figured at the heart of human achievements. While the history of the contributions made by seafarers and seafaring to the evolution of human civilization is a varied and fascinating subject, we must, of course, keep in mind that there is a vast range of human activity which has had little direct connection with seafaring.

OPPOSITE: Sir Ernest Shackleton's ship *Endurance* trapped in the Antarctic ice in 1915. Shackleton's expedition left England in August 1914. The aim was to cross Antarctica, but the ship became trapped in the ice floes of the Weddell Sea in 1915 and was eventually crushed. Shackleton and his party escaped in the ship's boats and were rescued by a Chilean tug. The challenge of the sea has induced many mariners to test themselves and their ships to the absolute limits, until finally, through improved technology and increased knowledge, all the oceans have been rendered navigable.

A major theme of the book will be the development of the maritime networks that have linked different societies and civilizations together, providing conduits for the exchange and distribution of goods, the projection of political and economic power and the diffusion of ideologies and cultures. In broad terms these networks can be characterized as either economic or political. Economic networks are essentially trading ones, which enable states or other organizations to extract, distribute, transform and consume resources such as food, metals or timber. Political networks are maritime empires or confederacies whose dominant groups direct the efforts of others to meet their own requirements. In practice the two categories have often overlapped. The most successful seafaring civilizations could be defined as those which have most effectively exploited economic and political networks to achieve their ends.

A distinction can, therefore, be made between certain dynamic, ambitious seafaring states and societies that have embraced the challenge of the sea and other more passive ones that have not striven for mastery and have been vulnerable to overseas domination. The more extensive the networks were the more difficult it was to use them to dominate other societies, because of the practical constraints on direct control over long distances. We shall see how improvements in technology, increases in resources and better social and political organization enabled seafaring civilizations to develop extensive maritime networks. For many centuries, however, the most extensive maritime networks were confined to certain geographical and cultural regions.

The end of the fifteenth century and the beginning of the sixteenth mark a watershed in the history of the seafaring civilizations of the world. It was in this period that several European nations began to expand their maritime networks across the Atlantic, Indian and Pacific oceans into regions where their political and economic power had previously been of little or no significance. This expansion is impressively symbolized by the famous voyages of Columbus, Vasco da Gama, Magellan and others. Ultimately the opening up of the global sea routes was to lead to the creation of a world-wide economic and political network. We shall explore some of the many repercussions of maritime expansion in a thematic and selective fashion.

The structure and scope of the main chapters is as follows. Chapter I surveys some major historical trends in seafaring technology. It looks at the evolution of ships and discusses the significance of ports and harbour installations and changes in the methods of maritime navigation. Particular attention is paid to the development of naval and merchant shipping used by those societies and civilizations whose seafaring activities, and their implications, are examined in the remaining chapters. Chapter II is concerned with the nature of maritime trading networks in major regions of the world, leading up to the watershed period of c.AD 1500. Chapter III focuses on political networks and maritime empires both before and after the period of dramatic European expansion. In chapter IV the emphasis is on how the development of seafaring networks has interacted with some of the world's major religions. Chapter V explores some of the major trends in the history of seafaring and civilization from the perspective of human diet and diseases. In chapter VI some general conclusions are reached on the basis of the previous chapters and a balance sheet of positive and negative aspects of the interplay between seafaring and civilization is outlined. The reading list which follows chapter VI is intended to provide some helpful starting points for further study of the subject matter of this book.

I

NAVIGATION

The origins of seafaring are lost in the mists of time. We cannot know with any certainty when, where or how the very first attempts were made to navigate some of the many open expanses of water which cover the majority of our planet's surface. What we can surmise, however, is that it was the need to find sources of food that encouraged our distant ancestors to find ways to pursue fish and other sea creatures and to seek edible plants and animals across those waters. The earliest boats were probably not used at sea, but on rivers and lakes. It is a significant step to risk travelling across the open seas, rather than on the relatively still waters of lakes or river estuaries, yet the earliest testimony to human achievements in seafaring is to be found, not in the remains of ancient sea-craft, but rather in the growing body of archaeological evidence of human habitation of islands and continents deemed to have been accessible to our ancestors only by sea. The sea crossings will probably have been made on some form of simple raft.

Archaeologists argue from what they know about the tools available to early humans and their use of suitable raw materials for other purposes, that a single log float, ridden astride, may well have been the earliest form of water craft. From this it is a logical and fairly simple step to fasten logs together in various ways (e.g. by binding or by pinning) and create a rudimentary prow. Comparison with craft known to be used in some areas of the world at present, or in the recent past, shows how effective such apparently primitive constructions can be as forms of water transport. Reed floats and boats are a very easy alternative to log-constructions, since they are essentially a bundle of reeds. Anthropologists and archaeologists have noted that such craft are found in central Africa, in the areas around Lakes Victoria, Turkana and Chad, a region which is associated with some of the earliest human remains. Egypt provides abundant evidence of their development, including a pictorial record. The popularity of such craft in the Nile valley must be partly due to relative lack of suitable timber. Traces of reed craft are found across the Mediterranean, in Europe, central Asia, Arabia and South Asia and even in Tasmania. Reed boats are found in several parts of South America today. Boats and canoes made from bark are also found in several areas, especially Australia and northern Europe, where there are very suitable trees including birch and beech.

Humans have used the skins of animals for a wide variety of purposes from Palaeolithic times, so it is hardly surprising that they developed this technology for seafaring. The evidence for animal skins as a major material for making ancient boats, canoes, rafts and floats is even more widespread. It ranges from fourth-millennium BC clay models of ships found in Mesopotamia and reliefs of rafts and floats carved on the palace walls of the Assyrian king Sennacherib (705–681 BC), to the *kayaks* and *umiaks* used by the Eskimos of Canada and Alaska. Skin boats and ships have great advantages in seas where the water is much colder, such as the North Sea or the Atlantic and Arctic Oceans, where their ability to remain dry and ship little water is important.

By far the most popular material for building seagoing ships was timber. From written sources it has been deduced that boats made of timber planks were used on the rivers of Mesopotamia in the middle of the third millennium BC. At about the same time, or soon after, planked craft were built in Egypt. By the middle of the second millennium BC the advantages of wooden plank construction, which enables ships to combine size, strength and flexibility, were being exploited widely in the Mediterranean, western Europe, the Near East and the Indian Ocean regions. Plank boats were used to some extent in all regions of the world, including pre-Columbian America and the Pacific Islands, but the chronology of their development is very hard to establish and the predominant types of sailing vessels in these areas seem to have been constructed from logs, rather than planks.

Mediterranean and Indian Ocean regions

Strong metal tools, initially made of bronze, were obviously a major element in the development of shipping technology. They were available in central Europe by the early fourth millennium BC and were introduced into the Mediterranean and Near East probably a little later. By the latter part of the third millennium BC wooden ships large enough to carry cattle were being used to ferry animals between the mainland and Cyprus. Oars and paddles were the methods of propulsion employed by the earliest seafarers, but by the end of the fourth millennium BC the sail was being used in the Mediterranean, the Red Sea and the Indian Ocean. We cannot say where or when it was first developed, although it seems likely that there were several, roughly simultaneous 'inventions' of the sail in these regions. The idea of attaching a broad wind-trap to a post or pole, fixed to the body of a ship, in order to use the wind to propel the vessel is taken so much for granted nowadays that we can easily overlook how ingenious and bold the concept must have seemed to those who saw it for the first time. The sailing ship is one of humankind's great technical innovations, to be ranked alongside the potter's wheel or the printing press in the history of civilization. Wooden sailing ships were to be the preferred means of maritime transport in the Mediterranean and adjacent regions for nearly two thousand years.

By the middle of the first millennium BC the two main methods of propulsion, sail and oars, were in widespread use across the Mediterranean region and beyond. Ship designs had begun to specialize according to function. The typical seagoing vessel of the first millennium AD might use oars or sails or both. There were many variations in the size, the depth, breadth and length of its hull, according to the needs of the ship's owner. The long, multi-level oared warship with a ram on its prow, best exemplified by the celebrated trireme and quinquereme (see Illustration 9, p. 84), is the type of vessel most readily associated with ancient seafarers. Yet these impressive-looking galleys with their huge crews of oarsmen were only for naval use. Less elegant, shorter, more rounded ships with a greater cargo capacity would have been commonplace in the harbours of the Mediterranean, the Red Sea or the Persian Gulf. Warships were far less specialized outside the Mediterranean, where rougher seas and stronger winds made the oared galley less effective and where naval activity was less regular.

The number of masts and the types of sails used by ancient mariners varied considerably, as did the techniques of building, rigging and sailing seagoing ships. By the third century AD the square sail was being gradually supplanted by the triangular, lateen sail, which, together with multiple oars, offered considerable advantages in the relatively calm conditions of the Mediterranean. A major advantage of the lateen sail is that it can be cut much larger and baggier than a square-cut sail, and thus it will catch and use the wind more efficiently, especially when sailing to windward. Exploitation of the monsoon winds, which was widespread from *c.*600 BC onwards, led to much larger, sturdier sailing vessels in the Arabian Sea and Indian Ocean. From an early stage, therefore, the shipbuilders of the Arabian Sea produced sewn plank boats with lateen rigged sails. These were the ancestors of the dhow, a term used by Europeans for a range of sailing vessels. Looking further afield it is not surprising that light, bamboo and timber craft with outriggers were very popular in South-east Asia, especially for use in shallow seas and among the islands.

In these seas and elsewhere experiments with sailing rig, steering methods and other aspects of seafaring gradually produced a diversity of ships built and sailed according to the dictates of local conditions. In general terms the factors influencing maritime ship design were similar throughout the world. They include the range of locally available materials, cargo sizes and weights, costs of crews (important for both merchant and naval requirements), the typical strengths of winds and currents and the depths of coastal waters. The interplay of these factors was complex. For example, larger cargo ships were produced where the cargoes were usually in bulk (e.g. timber, cloth, grain and cheaper metals), whereas smaller vessels might be favoured for luxury or high value cargoes (e.g. gold and ivory). But very large cargo ships were not common until more recent times, partly because individual merchants or ship owners lacked the resources and capital to produce them and run them effectively. Only the very rich or the ruling elites could afford to use them. A compromise was often sought in terms of mixing bulkier and smaller cargoes so that the typical merchant ship or trading vessel of the pre-industrial era was of a modest size and crew (see Illustration 6, p. 69 and Illustration 14, p. 142).

Northern and western Europe

The archaeological evidence indicates that from at least as early as the second millennium BC seagoing ships were making their way between the coasts of northern and western Europe, carrying people and goods over long distances. We have already noticed the importance of skin or hide boats in colder waters and it is clear from several Classical Roman writers that this type of vessel was considered highly suitable for the mariners of France, Ireland and the British mainland (see Illustration 13, p. 126). A framework of relatively slender timbers with hides stretched over it was also very light in weight, which was another useful feature for mariners who would often need to carry their craft over considerable distances and also be in need of extra buoyancy. Both sails and oars were used for propulsion, but very large oared galleys of the Mediterranean type were employed by the Romans only when their naval forces operated in northern waters.

Early medieval seafarers in north-western Europe and Scandinavia used the virtually double-ended vessels with upswept prow and stern characteristic of many later medieval craft. These features enabled the ships to be beached and launched easily and were useful when running before the wind, which seems to have been a favoured sailing technique. The building method was usually shell-first and consisted of light, overlapping planks, laid clinker-fashion, fastened to the keel by lashing, strengthened by strakes and attached to each other by iron clenches. By the ninth century AD Nordic shipwrights had developed a vessel type with a fairly broad keel that relied mainly on a single square sail for propulsion, with the oars being an auxiliary power source for use in calm weather or inland waterways. The typical Viking raiders' ship was a buoyant, fast sailing vessel that needed very little depth of water and few or no docking facilities.

Ship designs were adapted to suit the needs of the communities that used them. The Norwegian and Danish vessels that crossed the North Sea and the Atlantic were generally smaller than the Swedish ones that operated in the Baltic, sacrificing carrying capacity for seaworthiness in the harshest of conditions. By the thirteenth century the Scandinavians and their Germanic neighbours were using bulkier, less elongated ships for trade and even military activity. There were two predominant types, the hulk, or *hulc*, a word which originally seems to have meant something hollowed out like a peapod and was characteristically banana-shaped, with a curving hull, high prow and stern, but little or no sternpost or stempost. Side rudders were commonly used for steering. A good depiction of this type can be seen on the fourteenth-century seal of Winchelsea (see Illustration 6, p. 69). The hulk may have originated in the Low Countries, but it spread to England and across northern Europe and was the most common cargo vessel of the fourteenth and fifteenth centuries. The other was the cog, probably of Frisian origin, and distinguished by its angled prow and stern, flat bottom and high sides. The cog was the preferred vessel of the Hanseatic traders in the twelfth and thirteenth centuries. Both had a main square sail on a mast fitted amidships. Gradually larger sails and more masts were added. Stern-castles and fore-castles were used on both merchant and naval ships. One reason for the development of the hulk and the cog may be that harbour duties and maritime taxes encouraged merchants to use fewer, larger ships. Another reason may be the adoption of the centrally mounted stern rudder, gradually introduced to northern Europe in the twelfth and thirteenth centuries, which could be more easily incorporated in these types of ships. It has also been argued that high-sided sailing ships were more difficult for pirates to attack. By the sixteenth century, however, three-masted ocean-going vessels based on a sturdier, more flexible skeleton-first form of ship construction began to replace these earlier types.

The ships that launched European seafarers across the oceans of the world in the fifteenth and sixteenth centuries represent a combination of design and construction elements from the maritime traditions of the Mediterranean, the Indian Ocean and northern Europe. The caravels that were the favoured ships of the Portuguese in the fifteenth century had blunt, transom-built sterns with large rudders. They were carvel-built, that is with the planks joined edge-to-edge, rather than overlapping in the northern style. They could carry both square and lateen rigged sails, as Vasco da Gama's fleet did in his epic voyage to India, using the former style in the Atlantic, but converting to the latter style in the Indian Ocean.

Over the next few centuries the main developments in European shipping were in terms of size and speed. Sailing ships were made larger and sleeker, and were rigged with more masts and sails to use the available winds as effectively as possible (see Illustration 12, p. 117). Displacements of a

few hundred tons were typical of the ships of the late sixteenth century, but in later centuries ships displacing a
thousand tons or more were built. Bulk cargoes, carried
over long distances in large, fast ships also required protection. The Spanish, needing to transport the wealth of the
New World in large amounts and securely, developed the
most celebrated ship of the sixteenth century, the galleon, a
long, single- or double-decked, ocean-going ship with
sharply raised foredeck and quarter-deck and a hull pierced
with ports for heavy guns. It was the increasing number of
guns on the European warships of the sixteenth, seventeenth and eighteenth centuries that were to make them
particularly effective against the ships and coastal fortifica-
tions of the Orient. The Chinese, for example, had long
used artillery in warfare, but they did not employ large guns
on their ships (see Illustration 10, p. 96).

China

The seas of the Far East are far more windswept than the
Mediterranean, so the use of paddles and oars as methods
of propulsion did not override the importance of sails. The
earliest clear evidence of the use of fore and aft sails in
China dates to the third century AD, but it seems likely that
they were developed well before then, and simple, square

sails may have been in use some two thousand years earlier. The long coastline of China, punctuated by several major river estuaries, of which the Yangtze is the longest and broadest, gave rise to a myriad of seafaring communities. By the end of the first millennium AD they had evolved a variety of ships for use in both coastal and long-distance seafaring. The fruits of their experience produced the characteristic Chinese sailing ship, usually called the junk (from the word *jonq* used by Arab sources), which was suitable for both high seas and broad rivers like the Yangtze.

From the thirteenth and fourteenth centuries AD we have vivid descriptions of harbours thronged with seagoing ships by the Venetian traveller Marco Polo (1254–1324) and the widely travelled Arab geographer Ibn Battuta (1304–77). By combining European and Chinese written accounts with artistic and archaeological evidence we can put together a picture of the typical large trading vessels of fourteenth-century China. They were plank-built from pine or fir, using iron fastenings and a variety of caulkings, and they had internal, watertight bulkheads. They were equipped with from four to six masts and a complex set of sails made from both canvas and matting, stiffened with battens. The hull was gently curved, rather than entirely flat, but there was no keel and the stern ended in a broad vertical board, or transom, which easily accommodated a stern rudder, attached to a post. This latter invention seems to date from as early as the fourth century AD. The stern rudder, when combined with pivoted sails, which were much easier to adjust to the strength and direction of the wind than the standard riggings of the Arab and Western traditions, and other technical innovations, such as the drop-keel, or dagger board, enabled Chinese mariners to sail their junks very close to the wind and make very quick, precise changes in direction.

The beginnings of modern naval warfare

In the sixteenth century new types of fighting ships were developed in Europe. They were conceived as gunnery platforms, intended to stand off from their opponents and blast them to destruction. Consequently the designers of early modern warships focused on bringing as many guns to bear on the enemy as possible. Ships were made with multiple decks, low centres of gravity and very sturdy constructions. Tactics were evolved to take advantage of the broadsides that multiple guns could unleash. The 'line of battle' was developed for warships to sail past their targets, whether on sea or on land, and fire their powerful cannons from a suitable distance.

A celebrated early example of the changing face of naval warfare is the defeat of the Spanish Armada which attempted to invade England in 1588. The hundred or so English warships were mainly armed merchantmen, and included a large number of privateering vessels. Their captains were men such as Francis Drake, who had a wealth of experience in the running fights that ensued between pirates and their seaborne prey. There were also nineteen men-of-war that formed the core of the English navy. These ships were large, fast sailing vessels with plenty of guns. The English ships were generally much more manoeuvrable than those of the Armada. The range, power and quantity of the guns the English fleet could bring to bear were far greater than the weapons their opponents had to respond with. The Spanish fleet was made up of Mediterranean galleys, warships, armed merchantmen and hulks and was intended to proceed along the Channel, collect and transport a large army from the Low Countries across to England, against the prevailing south-westerly winds. It lacked a suitable base for concerted operations, its warships had insufficient long-range weapons to keep the English at bay and its commanders did not fully appreciate the hazards of conducting an operation of such magnitude and complexity in the face of a large, well-armed enemy fleet.

The English victory was as much due to the weather and the enemy's poor strategy as it was to the qualities of their own ships and seamanship, but it provided a taste of the kind of naval engagements that were to become commonplace as the emerging European maritime powers clashed at sea. The effectiveness of purpose-built warships with high-quality artillery was clearly demonstrated, as was the difficulty of mounting successful seaborne assaults against an enemy with a strong naval force at its disposal.

Throughout the seventeenth and eighteenth centuries the naval vessels of the major European powers grew in size and destructive power. The larger ships of the French and English fleets in the seventeenth century carried fifty, sixty or even seventy guns and displaced up to 2,000 tons. By the middle of the nineteenth century a top-rated ship of the line might carry 130 guns and displace 3,000 tons. With the introduction of iron and steel constructions and steam power in the nineteenth century, gradually superseded by diesel power in the twentieth century, truly gigantic battleships became possible, displacing up to 50,000 tons. Breech-loading, high-velocity guns enabled them to fight battles when ships were miles apart. Guided missiles and aircraft have extended these distances even further, but the principle of the warship as a floating gun platform is still essentially the same.

Steam power

The advent of steam-powered shipping did not revolution-ize seafaring overnight. Centuries of improvements in ship design and sailing techniques, coupled with the high levels of skill achieved by master mariners, meant that steam power had to improve considerably before it could chal-lenge the dominance of sail. Early steamships were driven by paddle wheels, a method of propulsion which was known to the Romans and used, in a limited way, by the Chinese in the twelfth and thirteenth centuries (see Illus-tration 11, p. 98).

The principle of the steam engine powered vessel was initially experimented with on lakes, rivers and canals in France, the United States and Scotland at the end of the eighteenth century. Traditionally the credit for building the first working paddle steamer is given to William Symington and Patrick Miller, whose *Charlotte Dundas*, named after her aristocratic patron Lord Dundas, towed barges along the Forth–Clyde canal in Scotland in 1801–2, but fears about the damage her wash might cause to the banks resulted in her being abandoned and left to rot. The river Clyde saw the launch of another early paddle steamer, the *Duke of Argyle*, which in 1814 completed a sea voyage to London by way of Dublin and Plymouth. By the 1820s they were to be found on rivers and seas around the world, although as seagoing ships they were disadvantaged by the need to have relatively slender hulls and to accommodate their bulky fuel, engines, boilers and paddles. These factors meant that they were not necessarily superior to many sailing ships, especially for long-distance trade and naval service.

The innovation which paved the way for the development of the large, fast merchant ships and warships of the twentieth century was the screw propeller. This method of harnessing the power of steam engines, as well as later forms of engine power, remains the principal one in use across the world. Its origins were very modest. In 1836 a farmer called Francis Pettit Smith used a screw propeller derived from a model boat to power a steam launch from the Thames Estuary to Folkestone. With financial backers and engineering partners he founded the Screw Propeller Company. Their ship, the *Archimedes*, demonstrated in 1843 that such a propulsion system could work on a steamship, but it was the celebrated I. K. Brunel who designed the first iron-hulled steamship deliberately fitted with a screw propeller. The *Great Britain*, built in 1843, managed 9 knots, but she was too slow and cramped to succeed as a competitive cargo ship. Nor was the Admiralty Board of the British Navy convinced of the superiority of the screw propeller, until in 1845 a contest was arranged between the naval ships HMS *Rattler*, fitted with a screw propeller, and a conventional paddle steamer of similar size and engine capacity, HMS *Alecto*. The latter was dragged astern against the motion of her paddles, graphically demonstrating the power of the screw propeller. In spite of the traditionalists' abhorrence at the prospect of piercing the hull of a ship below its waterline in order to propel it faster through the water, it was the steam-driven screw propeller which became the standard motive power of the Royal Navy's ironclad warships.

Further modifications were needed before steamships could effectively supplant sailing ships in the merchant marine and naval forces of the world. The engines had to be made smaller and more efficient, especially as the main fuel, coal, was both bulky and heavy (see Illustration 8, p. 80). It is estimated that from about 1850 to 1870 the proportion of the world's shipping that was propelled by steam rose from roughly 15 to about 50 per cent. Thereafter the steamship took over as the primary merchant vessel. The development of iron-hull construction techniques started in the nineteenth century, as the technological innovations

ABOVE: This photograph was taken in the 1870s, at a time when wooden sailing ships were being replaced by iron and steel steamships. The two vessels shown here, moored in the river Thames off Greenwich, are HMS *Fisgard*, a 'fifth-rate' Royal Navy ship built in 1813, and HMS *Arrow*, an iron gunboat of 1871.

of the industrial revolution made iron a suitable material for large-scale constructions. By the end of the 1880s around a quarter of the world's cargo vessels were sailing ships. Yet even as the iron steamships were growing in size, speed and popularity some of the most famous sailing ships of all were built and operated on the great transoceanic trade routes.

The tremendous increase in steam-powered shipping which occurred in the third quarter of the nineteenth century was, above all, a British phenomenon. While British ships already made up about 25 per cent of the world's steamer tonnage in 1850, by 1880 they accounted for over 50 per cent. In trading terms the British and their Empire dominated the maritime world. There were few ocean-going ships in the world at this time that did not visit British or British-controlled ports at least once in their life-spans.

Iron cladding for warships was experimented with in the early nineteenth century. The first proper iron warship was HMS *Warrior*, launched in 1860. In the last quarter of the nineteenth century the principal naval powers of the world gradually replaced their wooden sailing vessels with iron and then steel steamships (see Illustration 2, p. 26).

Ports

The earliest forms of seaborne transport did not require any special facilities on land, but once ancient civilizations began to trade regularly they developed harbours to accommodate ships more easily. The earliest evidence of man-made docks comes from India. At Lothal, in the Gulf of Cambay, archaeologists have found evidence of a rectangular basin with mud-brick walls and a wharf dating to the third millennium BC. Underwater excavations at the Indian site of Dvaraka have discovered what seems to be the remains of a harbour from the fifteenth century BC. There is also written evidence of dockyards in Egypt from a similar period. It is likely that most of the great maritime cities of the ancient Mediterranean and Indian Ocean regions had extensive quays and docks by the end of the first millennium BC. Within a short space of time large wharfs with cranes, warehouses, offices and the ancient equivalents of the buildings and machinery familiar to observers of the modern port were developed in many parts of the world. Changes in shipping produced appropriate changes in the size and nature of harbour technology, but basic features such as quays and warehouses have remained essentially the same for centuries. Probably the greatest difference between pre-industrial and modern ports is in terms of scale. Modern tankers and container ships are regularly berthed at harbours that are the size of small towns.

It is important to emphasize the interdependence between most coastal trading ports and their prosperous agricultural and commercial hinterlands in pre-industrial times. The port of Marseilles linked the farmlands and towns of France with the Mediterranean. Alexandria served not only the Nile valley, but also the countries of the Near East, which communicated with the city through the ancient caravan routes across the deserts. The Gulf of Cambay, where the ports of Lothal and Broach are situated, provided excellent access to the sea for the Gujerat region, the Indus valley and the food- and textile-producing areas of northern India. Going further north and inland one meets the main trade routes into central Asia. The Yangtze estuary has long been a major entry and exit point for the vast wealth of central China. The strategic significance of controlling ports for both trade and naval operations is another early development which continues to be important. Many naval battles have often been fought to gain or deny access to harbours.

Further modern developments that have had a major effect on ports are changes in the ways that goods and commodities are transported to and from ports. Canals linking major ports with rivers and inland centres were found in the Mediterranean, India and China in the first millennium BC. Railway and road links, however, are very much features of the industrial age. Their development means that populations and industries can be situated at great distances from the seaports that serve their needs. As a consequence the number of major trading ports around the world has decreased and the proportion of the world's population who have regular contact with the seafarers who service their trading needs has also declined, even in countries like the United Kingdom which depend heavily upon seaborne commerce (see Illustration 17, p. 202).

Finding the way at sea

The true art of navigation involves taking a ship from one place to another while out of sight of land. It is easy enough to go between two places that are within sight of each other, but once line of sight is lost a mariner must have some other way of determining in which direction to sail. The simplest method, not reliant on charts and instruments, is known as dead reckoning. In simple terms it is a continuous estimation of how far and in what direction(s) a ship has sailed from its point of departure. Even when a captain knows the typical performance of his ship very well, allowances must be made for variations in speed and direction caused by changes in sea conditions, currents and winds. It is possible, using dead reckoning, to make journeys of up to a few hundred miles across the open sea with some degree of reliability, although cumulative errors can easily result in missing the mark by a long distance. The more information a sailor has about the location of his destination and the nature of the seas to be navigated the better.

In ancient and early medieval times, when there were no definitive maps or charts, and when the precise reckoning of distances at sea was impossible, sailors relied heavily on personal experience and knowledge about the capabilities of their own ships, the typical behaviour of winds, tides and currents, the depths of inshore waters, the types of fish, birds and sea mammals found in particular waters, and the appearance of various coastal features. They supplemented this where necessary with the accumulated knowledge and experience of their fellow sailors. This kind of relative understanding of where places are and how they can be reached is exemplified by the following description of the position of Iceland, from the Icelandic *Book of Settlements* (*Landnámabók*), originally compiled in the twelfth century AD:

Wise men report that from Stad in Norway it is a voyage of seven days west to Horn in Iceland, and from Snaefellsnes (in western Iceland) it is four days' sail west to Greenland, at the point where the sea is narrowest. It is said that if one sails due west from Bergen to Cape Farewell in Greenland, one passes a half day's sail to the south of Iceland. From Reykjanes in southern Iceland it is five days' sail south to Slyne Head in Ireland, and from Langanes in northern Iceland it is four days northward to Svalbard in the Arctic Sea.[1]

This extract from the lengthy account of the settlement and early history of Iceland nicely illustrates some of the practical aspects of seafaring in the age before charts and navigational instruments. The reckoning of distances is made in terms of a unit notionally equivalent to a day's sailing. That does not imply the simplistic assumption that all ships would sail the same distance in the same amount of time. It has to be understood as a very rough and ready calculation, based on what a fast sailing ship aiming to make the journey might (optimistically) try to achieve, in fair weather and with very strong following winds. The figures given are a reasonable reflection of the actual distances in relative terms, with Iceland being roughly twice as far from the west coast of Norway as it is from the east coast of Greenland. In practice few ships could have hoped to make the crossings so quickly. The sailing times to Ireland and Svalbard (Spitzbergen) are particularly optimistic, but they seem to be taking account of the direction of the prevailing currents and main winds, which are predominantly good for westward journeys from Norway in spring and summer, but which can generally be relied upon to blow westerly in late summer and autumn. The places that are used as landmarks are mostly headlands. Snaefellsnes and Reykjanes are the names of the two smaller peninsulas on the southwestern coast of Iceland. The modern capital of Reykjavík is situated on the bay of Faxaflói, which lies between them. Slyne Head is a name used for the Mullett peninsula, on the western coast of Mayo. Even quite low-lying headlands can be seen from ten miles or so out to sea. For a novice it may seem very difficult to distinguish one headland along a stretch of coastline from any other, but there are subtle differences that the practised eye can easily spot. Experienced mariners would have built up an extensive personal memory bank of distinctive coastal features, which would enable them to tell when they had reached a particular point. Samples could also be taken of the seabed to establish what kinds of rocks, sand or mud lay beneath the ship's hull. Sounding, the practice of measuring the depth of water below a ship's hull, can be very helpful, not only in determining the likelihood of continued safe passage, but also in reckoning the position of a vessel. These forms of checking conditions and location are obviously more useful in waters where the depth changes greatly and the local geological conditions are also subject to considerable variation. Mediterranean seafarers made less use of them than those voyaging in the North Sea and the Atlantic Ocean.

The importance of local meteorological knowledge can be illustrated by the case of the celebrated monsoon winds. The main navigational importance of the seasonal monsoon winds, which alternate from East to West, is that they allow sufficiently sturdy ships to make swift, direct crossings of the Indian Ocean. They also encourage navigation along the littorals of East Africa, Arabia, India and the islands of South-east Asia. The main wind directions are from south-west to north-east between June and September, and from north-east to south-west between November and April. The origin of the name lies in the Arabic term *mausim*, meaning 'a season of winds'. The winds facilitate seasonal sailing voyages over great distances. Deciphering the pattern of the monsoon winds was a huge step forward in the maritime development of the Indian Ocean region. It was achieved by the middle of the first millennium BC, probably no later than *c*.600 BC, and allowed more direct trading across the Indian Ocean, between East Africa and India or India and South-east Asia. It also improved the maritime contacts between the Near East and the Mediterranean region and South Asia. Each area grew in knowledge of the other's peoples and their products and requirements.

The seamen of the Mediterranean eventually learned from experienced Indian Ocean seafarers how to predict and utilize them.

Later European sailors made similarly important discoveries. Increased knowledge of how to exploit the winds in the western Atlantic and the land breezes along the western coast of Africa played a significant role in the extension of Portuguese influence in the late fifteenth and early sixteenth centuries. Vasco da Gama made full use of the prevailing winds on his outward journey to the Cape of Good Hope in 1497. In 1611 a Dutch captain called Hendrick Brouwer discovered how to use the strong westerly winds from the Cape of Good Hope to run directly to the Sunda Straits between Sumatra and Java. Later voyages made with these 'roaring forties' winds occasionally took a ship too far to the east, and so the coast of Western Australia was sighted in 1616.

In all regions early seafarers used the celestial indicators to steer them on the right course. When visible, the stars were reliable guides once their patterns had been learned. The seasonal and latitudinal variations in the relative position and height of the sun at noon were understood by most of the seafaring cultures from quite early times, although there is a considerable gap to be assumed between

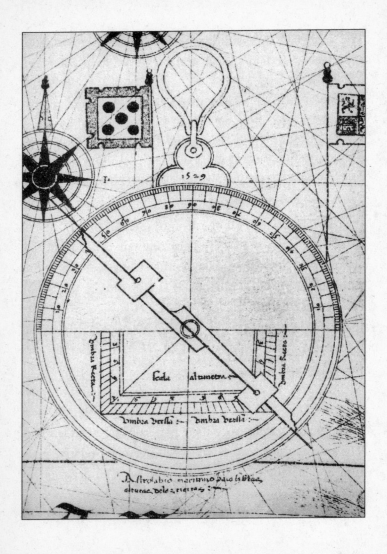

the level of appreciation of these phenomena contained in the written sources available to historians of ancient and medieval societies and the oral culture of the seafarers themselves. Celestial navigation is marginally easier in the Tropics because of the greater likelihood of the stars being visible and because of the relatively steady bearing of the stars in these regions. In more northerly latitudes all but the Pole Star seem to change their bearings as they travel across the sky. In the fifteenth century the use of the astrolabe among European mariners began. It was a reasonably accurate device for measuring celestial altitudes although it could only be employed on land or on a very calm sea.

The earliest use of the magnetic North Pole as a direction finder at sea is hard to establish. The magnetic properties of the lodestone were known to the Vikings, who used them as a navigational aid, but the earliest references to the mariner's compass in western Europe are to be found in writings of the late twelfth century. Traditionally it is the sailors of the Italian port of Amalfi who are credited with

OPPOSITE: A seaman's astrolabe, complete with ring and carefully graded measuring scale, drawn on a maritime chart of 1529. The advances in navigation represented by this kind of instrument were not the necessary precursors of maritime expansion, but they did help to give mariners greater confidence in their ability to exploit the enlarged trading networks.

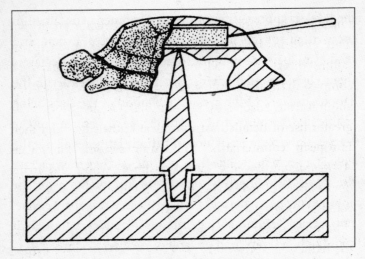

ABOVE: A reconstruction of a Chinese dry mounted compass of the kind described in twelfth- and thirteenth-century texts. The turtle was a cover for the magnet that controlled the needle's movements. It pivoted on a pin made of bamboo. Mariners preferred to use compasses floating in bowls of water.

the first use of the compass in Mediterranean seafaring. Like the Chinese, the Europeans found that a floating compass was very effective, but they gradually moved to mounting the needle on a brass pin and indicating the points on a card. By the fifteenth century compass navigation was commonplace in the European maritime world. Italian navigators developed a fairly accurate system for

finding their position in the Mediterranean and its immediate environs by using a compass, a chart and a list of
sailing directions. Arab navigators used the maritime
compass in the thirteenth century, probably having learned
about it from Europeans. In the Indian Ocean sailors made
greater use of detailed astronomical knowledge than their
European counterparts. The Arab system, known as
Al–Kemal, employed a *kamal*, a simple wood and string
device for measuring and checking the altitude of certain
celestial bodies using the same principles as the astrolabe.

An important development in the art of navigation was
the reduction of the units of time used to calculate a ship's
progress from 'days' to hours and, eventually, to minutes
and even seconds. The Venetians, expert makers of glass-
ware, produced high-quality hourglasses that were widely
used by the thirteenth century, but they were far from accurate. The famous thirteenth-century Catalan philosopher
Ramon Lull outlined a method for determining time according to the apparent movement of the 'Guards of the
Little Bear', two of the stars in the constellation which
circles the Pole Star, but it was subject to considerable
errors in its application, especially without specialized instruments. Even when mechanical timepieces became commonplace in the seventeenth century they still lacked the

accuracy required for precise navigation.

   With the publication of full sets of astronomical tables, which started towards the end of the fifteenth century, it was theoretically possible to determine one's position east or west of that point by a simple calculation involving the position of the sun at noon and the difference between the time at a fixed meridian of longitude, such as Greenwich, and local time. Every 15° of longitude east or west are the equivalent of one hour more or less than Greenwich Mean Time. In order to make such a calculation accurately, however, the navigator needed to know the precise time at Greenwich. Only then could a reliable calculation of longitude at sea be made. The solution to the problem of keeping an accurate record of Greenwich Mean Time for this purpose was addressed in various ways by the major seafaring nations of Europe. In a manner which seems curiously characteristic of the British combination of private enterprise, competition and state direction, a 'Board of Commissioners for the Discovery of the Longitude at Sea' was established by an Act of Parliament in 1714. It offered a prize of £20,000 for a system which was accurate to within thirty miles. Eventually, in 1765, the English clockmaker John Harrison (1693–1776) won the prize for his small but highly accurate chronometer, although the full award was withheld until the board was satisfied as to the general applicability of Harrison's watches. Captain Cook used a Harrison-designed watch on one of his voyages to the Pacific in 1775. Used in conjunction with the astronomical table and an accurate measuring device, such as the sextant, invented in 1757, the chronometer finally provided a truly accurate system for determining longitude and latitude. Working examples of the watch can still be seen in the National Maritime Museum at Greenwich. The acceptance of Greenwich as the prime meridian for such calculations did not occur until 1880, at a time when trading networks across the world were merging into one, and British maritime power was at its height.

Since the mid 1980s a completely different and far simpler system for establishing one's position at sea, or anywhere else on the surface of the globe, has been available. This is the Global Positioning System, or GPS. Twenty-four satellites placed in orbit around the Earth by the United States Department of Defense transmit signals to hand-held receivers which, by measuring the time differences between the signals received from three or more satellites, can provide a positional fix accurate to within a few metres or less.

II

TRADE

Trade can be defined as any transfer of goods or property which involves some kind of exchange. Long-distance trade is not a necessary or natural function of human societies, but its development is a common feature in the history of all urban civilizations. It seems reasonable to suppose that, just as humankind's first ventures in seafaring were motivated by the desire to obtain food from the sea, in the form of fish or mammals, so the earliest form of seaborne trade is likely to have been barter among small fishing communities for foodstuffs, raw materials and items such as clothing and tools. The links provided by long-distance maritime trading networks are a key element in the processes of economic and cultural diffusion and interaction, which can be said to have created the distinctive patterns of civilizations in the Mediterranean, the Near and Middle East, the Indian Ocean region and the Far East.

It was in the region known as the Fertile Crescent, principally in the valleys of the Nile, Euphrates and Tigris rivers, as well as in the Indus river valley, that the early urban civilizations arose and stimulated significant growth in maritime and terrestrial trade. Increasingly sophisticated agricultural techniques and organization enabled complex societies to flourish in these areas by the late fourth and early third millennia BC. Social differentiation and hierarchical stratification emerged, with the specialized functions of craftsmen, merchants, seafarers, warriors, priests, administrators and rulers becoming increasingly separate from those of the primary agricultural food producers. These groups encouraged and realized the growth of complex, interwoven land and sea trading networks, which furnished better and more diverse raw materials or manufactured goods for the consumer classes in the cities, palaces and temples of the Near East and India. Kingdoms and empires of varying sizes and power flourished in the second millennium BC. Similar developments occurred in China in the second millennium BC, but with greater emphasis on riverine rather than maritime trade.

Basic items such as food, animals and slaves, and more

sophisticated items such as perfumes, spices, precious metals and textiles were being regularly traded in ancient Mediterranean, Indian Ocean and Atlantic regions at local and regional levels several thousands of years ago. Some items can acquire a universal popularity, as a result of their availability through maritime trade networks, which is not at all connected to their practical value. Glass beads were undeniably an important export of South India and Mesopotamia for centuries. The attractive cowrie shells of the Maldive islands were even more widely appreciated. They functioned as decorations, status indicators, fertility symbols and a form of currency from central Africa to China.

Maritime trade in the Ancient Mediterranean

We can put together a reasonably clear picture of the patterns of maritime trade in the Mediterranean from the end of the second millennium BC, thanks to the increasing availability of written sources, in the form of official and private documents, monumental inscriptions and literary texts. The merchants of the Phoenician cities, and the Levantine coast in general, emerge as major figures in maritime trade from the second half of the second millennium BC. They were both encouraged and to some extent controlled by the larger states around them. Egypt to the south, the Hittites to the north and the Assyrians, Babylonians and Persians to the east demanded locally available materials such as timber and linen, locally manufactured goods, especially furniture, metal utensils and rich clothing and items obtained from trade with other places across the Mediterranean. These demands took the form not just of commercial trade but also of tribute, particularly in the first half of the first millennium BC, when the powerful Neo-Assyrian and Persian Empires dominated the Near East. The coastal cities of Tyre, Sidon, Byblos and Ugarit were home to thriving communities of craftsmen and traders, specializing in the import of commodities which were either traded on, or turned into luxury items for the temples and palaces of the Near Eastern cities. The harbours of the Levantine coast were occupied with the ships of these merchant middlemen, whose seafaring activities were a kind of essential lubricant to ensure the smooth operation of a wide range of commercial and also cultural exchanges between the societies of the region. The Phoenicians and their neighbours to the north and south never came together into a monolithic Levantine state, but were a group of cities and other settlements closely linked in political, economic and cultural terms, which depended upon maritime trade for a significant part of their revenues and their relative political independence. The merchants were organized into separate companies, but their dealings were loosely supervised by the rulers of the cities, who could tax goods passing through the harbours, but whose political power depended to a considerable extent on maintaining good relations with their principal customers, the larger, centralized states of the region.

The celebrated account of the voyage of the Egyptian priest Wenamon provides us with an insight into the nature of Mediterranean trade around 1100 BC. Wenamon was despatched from his home in Thebes to obtain the supplies of timber that he needed for a new ceremonial barge for the sacred image of Amon-Re. He journeyed from Tanis, in the Nile delta, to Byblos, but he was badly delayed in Dor, home of the notorious sea-raiders called the Tjekers, who robbed him of the precious metal items he was carrying to pay for the timber. He resorted to robbing some Tjekers himself in Sidon to recover part of his treasure, but he was still badly short of the riches needed to satisfy the ruler of Byblos as a down payment for the release of a cargo of cedar. In order to set the transaction in motion Wenamon had to arrange for his superiors to send gold and silver vessels, linen garments and mats, oxhides, ropes, lentils and fish. This combination of luxuries and staples is probably typical of the cargoes which were traded between Egypt and Phoenicia, and which the merchants of Byblos could either find uses for themselves, or pass on to others through sales or gifts.

The Levantine traders' prosperity and cultural influence grew as their powerful neighbours expanded their empires and put even greater demands on their capacity to supply goods and raw materials. The eighth century BC saw an expansion of the already quite extensive seaborne trading network of the Phoenicians beyond the Eastern Mediterranean and the foundation of numerous overseas settlements along the coasts of Spain, Sardinia, Sicily and North Africa. One of these, Carthage on the coast of Tunisia, became a powerful state in its own right, but most developed as outposts of Levantine culture, whose interaction with the local inhabitants helped to encourage the development of urbanization, state formation, complex social hierarchies and sophisticated commercial activities. The Greeks owed their alphabet and probably many of their early political and economic institutions to contacts with the Phoenicians. They are credited in turn with a major role in the growth of urban civilization in Italy, and the rise of the wealthiest and most powerful of ancient civilizations: Rome.

Greeks and Romans

The Greeks had traded across the Mediterranean in the Bronze Age, but the scale of Greek involvement in long-distance trade appears to have dramatically declined from *c.*1200 BC, in what scholars refer to as the Dark Age of Greek history, reviving only in the eighth century BC, when Greek traders are found alongside Phoenicians, Syrians, Etruscans and others at places like Al-Mina on the coast of Syria and Pithekoussai (Ischia) in the Bay of Naples. The renewed growth of Greek trade in the Mediterranean was stimulated by the development of numerous small, independent urban communities, similar to those of the Levant. These city-states traded freely by sea with each other and with the rest of the Mediterranean, encouraged by the relative ease with which goods and commodities could be moved between the numerous small bays and inlets which made natural harbours.

A great deal of the archaeological evidence of Greek and Roman trade is most obviously furnished by ceramic remains, such as painted vases and amphorae (storage jars), which indicate the presence of traders who were of Greek or Roman origin, or those who were in close contact with the Greeks and Romans. These ceramics do not necessarily represent the main items of trade. They may be containers for bulk commodities such as wine or fish sauce, or they may be goods of moderate value such as painted pottery, which accompanied luxury items, functioning partly as ballast.

Some places developed a speciality in particular products, for example glass from Egypt, fine textiles from Kos, oil from Athens, fish from the Black Sea, grain from Sicily. Specialized markets emerged, whether because of their location on trading routes or near to sources of supply and demand, or because of favourable political conditions. Thus Corinth was from early times a focus for overland and seaborne trade. Hellenistic Rhodes profited from her position between the Levant and the Aegean, and from her close links with Egypt, becoming a major grain market. Delos, which had the status of a free port after 166 BC, was a very important centre for the slave trade. Alexandria flourished under Ptolemaic and Roman rule as one of the main links between the trading networks of the Indian Ocean, Asia and the Mediterranean.

The movement of goods, commodities and slaves without exchange, whether through war, piracy, non-reciprocal gift-giving or tribute, was also an important aspect of ancient economic activity. Navies and pirates might occasionally interfere with the seaborne trade of the

Mediterranean, but they rarely caused any long-term disruption. It was not in the interests of the inhabitants of the region to discourage merchants from carrying their cargoes from city to city. A substantial part of the Greek and Roman slave trade was supplied from prisoners of war, or the victims of piracy, and in the second and first centuries BC the Romans acquired large quantities of grain from their provinces of Sicily and Africa as tribute. Nevertheless the economic world of the ancient Mediterranean can be characterized as one in which maritime trade was highly developed and, especially at the height of the Roman Empire, it was an integral part of Classical civilization.

Most coastal cities built commercial harbours with quayside facilities, including warehouses and offices for merchants and magistrates. Within a large city there might also be specialized marketplaces, such as the fish market at Athens or the slave market in Alexandria. The Romans were great civil engineers whose creative energies were channelled into both impressive and practical building projects. They even developed a form of concrete which would set underwater and this led to the creation of commercial harbours on a grand scale at places such as Leptis Magna on the Libyan coast, Caesarea in Palestine and Ostia, the port of Rome, at the mouth of the river Tiber. The easy movement of bulk goods by sea both encouraged and was encouraged by the proliferation of large-scale urban centres and the needs of a standing army in excess of 250,000 men. The city of Rome probably had a population of over one million in the first to fourth centuries AD. Its immediate agricultural hinterland was not capable of feeding it, however, and to sustain its inhabitants seafaring merchants imported grain, wine and other staples from Spain, Africa, France, Sardinia and Sicily and other parts of the Mediterranean.

Long-distance trade was mostly carried out on a small scale by professional traders who either received items directly from the producers, in return for money or other goods, or bought them from other merchants, and then passed them on to the consumers, again in return for payments in money or in kind. Much of this trade was speculative and traders might have to visit several places in the attempt to dispose of their cargoes. In literary sources the typical trader is a free person of moderate wealth who moves from one market to another, buying and selling a range of goods in varying quantities. He may also have his own ship, but many traders formed temporary partnerships with ship owners. Both the Greeks and the Romans had a strong social prejudice against traders, who were considered inferior in moral and social terms to landowners. The Romans attempted to legislate against a high level of involvement in maritime trade among their aristocracy, limiting the size of ships which senators could own. It seems that although such laws were aimed at maintaining the image of a ruling aristocracy which was above the petty affairs of merchants, in practice the wealthy landowners of the Roman Empire were heavily involved in maritime trade, operating through semi-independent middlemen. Roman shipping merchants formed associations for religious and social purposes and they were encouraged to pass their businesses on to their heirs by imperial authorities conscious of the need to maintain the flow of seaborne commerce.

In many parts of the ancient Mediterranean women's involvement in trade was circumscribed by laws or customs which prevented or hindered them from carrying out large-scale transactions without male supervision. They are most often found trading food, small items of clothing and especially perfumes, which were considered appropriate goods for females. Women do occasionally feature in the documentary sources carrying out business on a larger scale, often through agents, especially from the third century BC onwards, when more women began to acquire independent wealth and so gained access to the economic activities which went with it.

Slaves and freedmen too were often closely involved in maritime trade, both as assistants to free persons and as semi-independent agents. Some of the most fascinating accounts of trade disputes from the law-court speeches of Classical Athens involve slaves or former slaves. The Romans freed very large numbers of slaves who did, in some cases, make themselves very wealthy from commercial activities. One of the early ancient novels, by Petronius Arbiter, describes the fictional rise of Trimalchio, a freed slave who inherited enough from his former master to go into the shipping business:

> To cut a long story short I built five ships, got a cargo of wine, worth its weight in gold in those days, and sent them to Rome. Every single ship was wrecked; you would think it was a put-up job. That's the truth, I'm not making it up. In one day Neptune swooped thirty millions. Was I downhearted? No, I assure you, I felt the loss as if it was nothing. I built some more, bigger and better, more successful, and everybody said I was an intrepid fellow. You know, a big ship has a lot of staying power. Once again I shipped wine, bacon, beans, Capuan perfume, and slaves … There's no delay when the gods are on

to something. In one trip I rounded off a good ten million. I promptly bought up all my patron's estates. I built a house, I bought slaves and livestock; whatever I touched grew like a honeycomb.[1]

Trimalchio's story is exaggerated for literary effect, but it vividly conveys the risk, excitement and potential for gain inherent in maritime trade for individual merchants. The scale of some aspects of maritime trade was larger in the heyday of the Roman Empire (31 BC–c.AD 400) than it had ever been before, as can be seen from the evidence of processing and distribution installations, discarded storage containers (amphorae) and wrecked merchant ships. Bulk cargoes of grain, wine, oil and other staples were taken in fleets of merchant ships between major collection and distribution points, for both state and private customers.

The trends outlined above for maritime trade were, in general terms, repeated in other parts of the world. The gradual growth of powerful states and stable, sophisticated economic systems encouraged maritime (and, of course, terrestrial) trade. By the middle of the first millennium AD most areas of what we call the Old World were linked in extensive trade networks, many of them maritime. While only the shipwrights, sailors and maritime traders were totally dependent upon seafaring for their livelihoods, it is true to say that maritime networks promoted and helped to maintain highly diverse social structures in which individuals and groups were able to specialize in economic, religious, military and cultural tasks. It is important to emphasize the role of staples in the expansion of this trade. A great deal of it was bulk cargoes of food, raw materials such as metals and timber, cloth, aromatics and spices which were so thoroughly embedded in the urban cultures of many places in Europe, the Mediterranean, the Near and Middle East, South and East Asia, that they can be considered part of the fabric of civilization.

Indian Ocean

The Indian Ocean region and the Mediterranean were closely linked by caravan routes across Arabia and between the Near East and the Middle East. The development in South Asia of large states and imperial regimes in the first millennium AD gave added impetus to the growth of urban civilizations in areas which were linked by the trading networks of the Indian Ocean region, where the exchange of goods, wealth, technology and ideas stimulated the dominant groups to tax peasants and organize local markets and trading networks. They also promoted greater production in farm, forest and hillside and encouraged people to exchange the results for precious metals and imported goods which could be deployed to sustain governments, craftsmen, and religious and cultural elites similar to those already established among the more sophisticated trading partners. Hence urban civilizations grew up around the edges of the Near East, the Horn of Africa and South-east Asia, partly in response to the stimulus provided by maritime trade.

Maritime economic trade between the Mediterranean, the Near East and the Indian Ocean region was helped by the relative prosperity and stability of the Roman (later Byzantine) Empire, although Rome was at a disadvantage due to the position of its main rival, the Persian Empire, first under the Parthians and from the third to the seventh centuries AD under the Sasanians. The Sasanians gradually extended their control over key parts of the Arabian Peninsula, especially Dhofar and Oman. As early as the first century AD the Romans were aware that their balance of trade with South Asia and China was not good, as is indicated by comments made in his *Natural History* by the Elder Pliny, who died in the eruption of Vesuvius in AD 79. From the Persian point of view Roman gold and silver made the Indian Ocean traders more prosperous and, therefore, better able to trade with the Persian Gulf and its immediate hinterland. When the flow of Roman gold declined in the fifth century AD due to the partial collapse of the Empire, the Indian Ocean merchants increased their interest in the gold-rich lands of South-east Asia.

Aksum is an interesting example of a civilization which benefited from its integration into the Indian Ocean trading networks. It was the first urban civilization in Africa south of the Nile valley and its period of greatest prosperity dates from the first century BC to the seventh century AD. The Aksumites traded extensively with the civilizations of the Mediterranean, via Egypt, and with Arabia and India. The increasing volume of trade along the monsoon-aided sea routes between India and the Red Sea can be seen as one of the reasons behind the rise of Aksum. An aggressive stance on trading led to wars and political domination of parts of Somalia and south-western Arabia from the second century to the fourth and fifth centuries AD, when they were also christianized. Aksum had a significant merchant marine and a naval fleet which allowed it to dominate the Red Sea, exploiting its controlling position on the Gulf of Aden. Its chief port was Adulis, which, in the sixth century AD displaced the Yemenite trading ports of Saba and other small kingdoms as the main entrepôt for the trade between India and Egypt.

In the period before the rise of Islam maritime trade to the south of the Red Sea focused on Yemen (resins such as frankincense and myrrh) plus Ethiopia and Somalia (gold, ivory and resins). Gradually much of the East African coast was linked into the trading networks of southern Asia. The trading ventures of the merchants of the Yemen, and later those of Aksum, along the coastline to the south of the Horn of Africa were not as frequent or as mutually influential as those which linked them to the Mediterranean and South Asia. This is because the settlements that they visited in Somalia and Kenya were not part of large states, nor were they linked to complex urban cultures in their hinterlands. They did not produce sophisticated goods, but rather they provided raw materials such as ivory and rhinoceros horn.

The extent of the maritime trading network of the Indian Ocean region in the first millennium AD was impressive. It effectively stretched from the margins of the Mediterranean and Mesopotamia and the shores of East Africa in the north and west, to the islands of South-east Asia and the South China Sea in the east. At the heart of this region were the merchants and seafarers of South Asia and Arabia. Their ports and ships were filled with the produce and the wealth of a multitude of lands and peoples.

The predictable regularity of the monsoon was a great benefit for merchants. While the winds might vary in their strength (the south-west wind was particularly stormy) and sailing was not always possible, they were reliable from season to season, enabling long-distance voyages to be undertaken to exploit trading connections with far-away places on a regular basis. As a consequence it was possible to place greater emphasis on the regular acquisition of materials and products from distant lands, and to depend to a greater extent on distant markets for one's own products, or those acquired through trade. The long seasons could not easily be diverged from, so certain trading ports had to remain relatively quiet for those months of the year when the winds were not favourable, and the exchange of goods tended to take place within the confines of the monsoon-determined rhythm. Only the advent of steam power really brought an end to this pattern. It is also worth noting that the monsoon rains determined a lot of the agricultural production of these regions, so that the rhythms of human existence on both land and sea were similarly dictated by the elements.

The historian Kenneth McPherson has emphasized the extent to which the 'balance of trade' in this region was very favourable to South Asia: 'Put most simply, South Asia exported a greater value of goods than it imported, with the result that huge quantities of gold and silver flowed into the subcontinent.'[2] Although a lot of the gold acquired by the elites of India came overland from central Asia and Siberia, in the first millennium AD it arrived in substantial quantities from the Mediterranean, from East (and indirectly West) Africa, and increasingly from South-east Asia, to where the merchants of South Asia were attracted in large numbers at the start of the first century AD.

South-east Asia and China

The development of maritime trade networks in South-east Asia is likely to have been a spontaneous result of the combination of increased population density, greater social and economic differentiation and a well-developed indigenous maritime technology. It was a region where, from the earliest times, seafaring had been an important means of travel and communication. Soon after the rise in sea levels at the end of the Pleistocene era the growing of rice and other crops and the exploitation of domesticated animals such as pigs and chickens spread throughout the region. By the end of the first millennium BC merchant ships from South-east Asia were visiting the ports of China and India, exchanging indigenous products such as cloves, rice and tin for Chinese silks, bronzes, Roman gold and Indian cotton. The growth of urban civilization was slower in this region than in China or South Asia, and state-formation was primarily the result of improvements in agricultural productivity and the collection of surpluses as well as the development of craftsmanship in metals and ceramics. Yet it seems likely that the establishment of maritime trading links with the Indian Ocean, China and the Mediterranean encouraged the creation of coastal trading states among the islands and on the deltas and estuaries of some of the larger rivers. Over the course of the next millennium maritime commercial interaction across the Indian Ocean and from South-east Asia to China increased, undoubtedly prompted by the growing demands in the cities and palaces of these regions for a wide range of products and goods. By the ninth century AD Chinese merchants had begun to penetrate the harbours and markets of South-east Asia and India. Arabian and Persian merchants travelled further southwards along the east coast of Africa, getting as far as Mozambique and Madagascar, where they encountered the descendants of Malaysian settlers.

In the first and early second millennia AD Chinese maritime trade expanded in response to a variety of factors. There was both an increase in the demand for imported goods and in the market for Chinese exports, both of which were stimulated at very basic levels by the growth of the Chinese economy. The population of China nearly doubled under the T'ang and Sung dynasties, rising to in excess of 100,000,000 by the end of the twelfth century AD. The increased population was fed by more intensive exploitation of the agrarian resources, not only in terms of the methods of cultivation but also in the organization and control of peasant labour, though the relationships between landowners and tenants, and between workers and merchants, were to be an almost constant source of internal unrest. There was also a shift in the balance of the population away from the vulnerable northern provinces towards central and southern China. Production of metals increased, as did that of textiles – not just silk, but hemp and cotton. The production of high-quality ceramics grew and the techniques were refined, achieving the levels of perfection which made Chinese porcelain the envy of much of the civilized world.

Maritime commerce across the Indian Ocean and from South-east Asia to China increased steadily, undoubtedly prompted by the growing demands in the cities and palaces of these regions for a wide range of products and goods. By the ninth century Chinese merchants had begun to penetrate the harbours and markets of South-east Asia and

India. The unprecedented era of peace and stability in China under the Sung dynasty (960–1279) was a period of great economic growth, focused on internal agriculture, crafts and trade, but also featuring a flourishing overseas trade, dominated by Chinese shipping, with South and South-east Asia. Chinese participation in maritime trading networks developed rapidly from the eleventh century onwards as products of the highest quality in ceramics, textiles (especially silks) and metalwork were carried across the seas to be exchanged for gemstones, spices, grains and textiles (especially cotton).

The sheer volume of foreign trade in the Sung period is impressive. Records are available for the state's income from customs duties on maritime trade, levied at rates varying from 10 to 40 per cent, depending on the nature of the items being imported. In the tenth century the amounts being raised were fairly modest, only about 500,000 strings of 1,000 cast bronze coins, but by the end of the eleventh century this had risen to 65,000,000 strings. By the early twelfth century the duties amounted to around 20 per cent of total government income. The Mongol conquest in the thirteenth century caused little disruption to maritime trade, notwithstanding their overseas expeditions, including an invasion of Japan in 1281 that was broken up by a storm that went down in Japanese legend as the 'Divine Wind' (*kamikaze*). Nor did the Mongols do anything which interfered with the growing expansion of Chinese traders into South-east Asia, particularly Vietnam and Malaysia. Indeed, their expeditions to Vietnam, Cambodia and Java may even have improved commercial relations between southern China and these areas, paving the way for even more ambitious expeditions under the early Ming rulers. In the fourteenth and early fifteenth centuries China was the dominant maritime power, both commercially and militarily, in the South China Sea.

Pre-Columbian America and Oceania

Two regions of the world need to be excepted from the general pattern described above, but for different reasons. It is very clear that there were extensive maritime and terrestrial trading networks in the Americas prior to the arrival of Europeans at the end of the fifteenth century. The islands and bays of the Caribbean in particular were a natural arena for maritime communications. Flints, pottery, stone beads and pendants are among the items of maritime exchange that have survived in the archaeological record from the Caribbean. Metals, obsidian, textiles and cacao beans also seem to have been traded by sea over considerable dis-

ABOVE: Log rafts with square and fore-and-aft sails from Peru. It was in the shape of sailing craft like these that the Conquistadors had their first encounters with the maritime trade of the Americas.

tances. Early Spanish expeditions often encountered sea-going vessels, mainly rafts and canoes. Much of this trade was focused on the major urban civilizations in Central America.

A good example of the diversity of goods carried in Mesoamerican maritime trade can be obtained from the description of a native maritime trading expedition encountered off Honduras by Columbus on his fourth voyage in 1502:

Our men brought the canoe alongside the flagship, where the admiral gave thanks to god for revealing to him in that moment, without any toil or danger to our people, all the products of that country. He took aboard the costliest and handsomest things in that cargo: cotton mantles and sleeveless shirts embroidered and painted in different designs and colours ... long wooden swords with a groove on each side where the edge should be, into which were fastened with cord and pitch, flint knives that cut like steel; hatchets resembling the hatchets used by other Indians, but made of good copper. For provisions they had such roots and grains as the Indians of Hispaniola eat, also a wine made of maize that tasted like English beer.'[3]

In this respect the maritime trade networks of pre-Columbian America are similar to those of the Old World. The major difference is that there does not seem to be any significant evidence of inter-regional trade.

Human beings probably began to settle the islands of South-east Asia about 100,000 years ago. Having developed sufficient maritime skills to be able to navigate across the shallow seas they came to Indonesia, Borneo, New Guinea and Australia no later than about 35,000 years ago. The most adventurous group, the Malayo-Polynesians, eventually settled the islands off the East African coast and in the Pacific Ocean, including the most remote of all habitable places, Easter Island. The settlement of Melanesia and Polynesia seems to have occurred much later than the Southeast Asian archipelagos, long after the inhabitants of New Guinea had developed agricultural techniques and domesticated both plants and animals. Their characteristic pottery, derived from the Lapita style of the Moluccas, has been found as far east as the Marquesas Islands, on a line of longitude 140° west of Greenwich, nearly 5,000 miles north-west of Australia. Moving from one island group to another, probably sailing in light, wooden boats or canoes with single or double hulls and outriggers for stability, they had got as far as Fiji by c.1300 BC. During the first millennium BC they made their way into the Polynesian Islands. The various island groups of the South Pacific, including New Zealand, were all settled by about the thirteenth century AD and this fact alone indicates that there was some maritime communication between them. Significant maritime trade networks are not easily demonstrated, however, and it seems that the island groups developed fairly independently of each other, until the arrival of Europeans in the seventeenth, eighteenth and nineteenth centuries.

The case of Australia is even more unusual in that, after

the initial settlement, which was clearly seaborne, there was no development of maritime trade or major exploitation of marine resources, because the resources of the land, rivers and coast were sufficient for the population. Australia was not significantly linked to the world of the Indian Ocean until the arrival of Europeans in the eighteenth and nineteenth centuries. Its indigenous peoples had no regular contacts with other cultures, because outside visitors were few and within Australia seafaring was limited to coastal waters.

Medieval European maritime trade

The collapse of the Roman Empire in the west in the fifth century AD and the Muslim advance into the Mediterranean in the seventh century, both had major disruptive effects on maritime trade. They did not, however, cause a complete cessation in the seaborne commerce of any part of the Mediterranean or the Atlantic and North Sea networks that had developed on the fringes of the Roman world. Political stability, large cities and standing armies had provided encouragement for mercantile activity in terms of its scale and intensity, but they were not essential for the continuation of mercantile communications. As the peoples of Christendom and Islam created new cities and

ABOVE: The fourteenth-century seal of the English port of Winchelsea is a vivid symbol of the pride that medieval European states and towns took in their maritime commerce. The ship depicted is a hulk. It has the distinctive rounded hull, stern and forecastles and steering oar. In this scene of departure on a trading venture the anchor is being raised by a windlass to the accompaniment of a trumpet fanfare.

states, they established new trading networks and renewed old ones. We shall look more closely at the nature of trade in the Muslim world in chapter IV, but the next phenomenon to consider here is the development of mercantile empires of the Hanseatic League and the Republic of Venice.

The idea behind the Hanseatic League was first floated in the northern German port of Lübeck in the thirteenth century, at a time when the Teutonic knights were 'pacifying' the Baltic littoral. It was based on the control of strategic ports linked into a network which, while it may have been initially envisaged as a political and military one, developed as a maritime trading empire. It is perhaps better to call the Hanseatic League a confederacy, since it had no clear hierarchical structure, all major decisions being taken collectively at meetings of an assembly called the *Hansetage* in Lübeck, which first met in 1356. Its large number of members, around 100 ports and trading centres stretching from the southern coast of Finland to the Rhineland, enabled it to dominate key items of trade and trade routes. The trading network of the Hanseatic League was very extensive, reaching from the Baltic into the North Sea, the Atlantic and even the Mediterranean, via key ports such as Lisbon, Malaga, Valencia and Venice. The essential framework was in place by the middle of the fourteenth century. In major ports such as Bruges, London, Bergen and Novgorod there was a Hanseatic *kontor* (counting house). The *kontoren* were small enclaves of Hanseatic power within the cities, rather like modern embassies or consulates, but with a narrow, trading focus. The Bruges *kontor*, for example, was established in 1323 and was the focus of northern European trade in textiles, grain, fruit, wine, spices and many other commodities from the Baltic, Atlantic and Mediterranean carried by the seafaring merchants of the Hanse.

Although they could muster or purchase considerable naval and military resources when pressed, it was the collective bargaining power of these merchants that was the basis of their influence. They negotiated tax concessions and monopolies on the major items of maritime trade between selected ports. If a new, profitable trade began to emerge they moved in to dominate it. In the fifteenth century, for example, the English were driven out of the excellent fishing waters off Norway by the requirement that only Hanse members be allowed to export from the central Staple in Bergen. The English transferred their attentions to Iceland, providentially improving the quantity and regularity of maritime trade between the Icelanders and the rest of Europe, at a time when their traditional providers in Norway were more interested in sailing south-west, rather than north-west. Later in the fifteenth century pressure from within the Hanseatic League to maximize its revenues from fishing led to the English being squeezed out again. This time they moved even further west, opening up a route to the rich fishing grounds off the coasts of Labrador and Newfoundland.

The priorities and the principal methods of constraint applied by the League were economic, rather than political. It did not seek to control entire states and territories, only the key ports and markets, and the main items of maritime trade exchanged between them, such as grain, timber, cloth, fish and wine. An early manifestation of the Hanseatic approach occurred in 1284, when the Norwegian king, Erik II (the Priesthater), tried to curb the activities of the north German merchants who were increasingly dominating Norwegian internal trade. He swiftly discovered that the same merchants and their associates had the ability to starve his country into surrender by blockading the grain trade that Norway depended upon. An indemnity, freedom from taxation and unlimited access to ports south of Bergen were the price for lifting the blockade.

Gradually, however, the collective power of the Hanse diminished in the face of the rise of strong nation states, whose economic development the Hanseatic League had to a considerable extent assisted, but whose rulers could no longer tolerate an independent maritime confederacy operating within their accepted spheres of influence. In the sixteenth and seventeenth centuries the power of the Hanse succumbed to a combination of internal disruption and external pressure, both to some extent originating from the political and economic activities of strong, increasingly centralized states such as England, Sweden and Habsburg Spain. For example, the Swedish kings employed their new naval forces in a contest with those of Lübeck in the latter part of the sixteenth century, to wrest control of the Gulf of Finland. Hanse merchants were too vulnerable to this and other navies to resist the pressure to accept national sovereignty. The last meeting of the *Hansetage* was held in 1669, but only eight members bothered to send a representative.

The city of Venice was established in the sixth century AD when the Ostrogoths were overrunning northern Italy. Its position on the island in the lagoon to the north of the Po delta was chosen as a refuge from war, but it was to provide an almost ideal location from which to establish a maritime trading empire. In its early stages Venice provided an important link between the eastern and western halves of the Mediterranean. The two halves had been closely integrated both politically and economically by the Roman

Empire, but the links between them were severely disrupted by the disintegration of Roman power under pressure from barbarian and Muslim armies and internal problems. As the kingdoms and caliphates of the Mediterranean region began to settle into a set of relatively stable political relationships, allowing the development of extensive trading networks, the Venetians emerged as major carriers of seaborne commerce between both Christian and Muslim ports. The Venetians obtained favourable terms for trading with Constantinople in 1081 and similar concessions from the new Crusader states of the Levant in the twelfth century. Even after the fall of the Latin kingdoms in the east the Venetians maintained strong interests in trade between Egypt, the Levant and the rest of the Mediterranean. Spices, especially pepper, silks and sugar were among the leading trade items the Venetians shipped back to the Adriatic and on to other parts of Europe. In return they offered northern European products like woollen textiles and their own speciality, glass, to their trading partners.

In 1202 the Fourth Crusade was undertaken with the support of Venetian shipping as well as other resources. It got into immediate difficulties when the Venetians demanded payment for the large number of ships they had built for the crusading army that was too small and too impoverished to argue. In part payment the crusaders joined with Venetian forces in an attack on the Christian port of Zadar on the Dalmatian coast, in furtherance of Venice's strategic aim of control of the Adriatic. Consequently the exasperated Pope Innocent III (1198–1216) was obliged to excommunicate an entire crusading army. The next stage in the campaign was a voyage to Constantinople, to install a pretender on the Byzantine throne. In circumstances that seem to have been more accidental than planned, the Frankish and Venetian forces took complete control of the city and inaugurated a short-lived eastern version of the Holy Roman Empire.

The unrepentant Venetians' share of the spoils was a privileged position in Constantinople, complete with dock-yards, plus a selection of lucrative territorial possessions covering the trading routes of the eastern Mediterranean, of which the island of Crete, situated at the confluence of sailing routes from Africa, the Aegean, the Levant and Egypt, was the most important. They held it until the Ottomans drove them out of Candia (Heraklion) in 1669. Venetian naval power ensured territorial control over Istria and the key ports of the eastern Adriatic as well as the enclaves in Crete, the Ionian Islands and the Aegean. Other coastal cities established commercial and military outposts and competed with Venice, particularly Genoa and Pisa, but none attained the same level of naval and mercantile domination. Through assiduous nurturing of the sources of her mercantile wealth Venice became one of the great maritime cities of the world.

The naval dominance of Venice was based upon a fleet of light galleys. They were superficially similar to those of earlier Mediterranean navies, but they were ideally suited to a style of marine warfare in which fighting at close quarters with small guns and other missile weapons became the norm. They could also bring their personnel and weaponry close to shore-based opponents. Most important of all the republic had a large number of naval vessels permanently available (up to 146 in 1581) and could easily commission more and supplement them with mercenary or allied forces. The standing navy of the Venetians was on a scale not seen in the Mediterranean since the height of the Roman Empire. It enabled the Venetians to pursue a vigorous policy of suppressing 'piracy', although this was perhaps more of an aspiration than a realistic goal, espe-

OPPOSITE: Venice in a woodcut of 1486, by E. Reuwichs, showing some of the grand architecture that was built on the profits of the Venetian trading empire. The vessel in the foreground is a light galley of the kind used by Venice's navy.

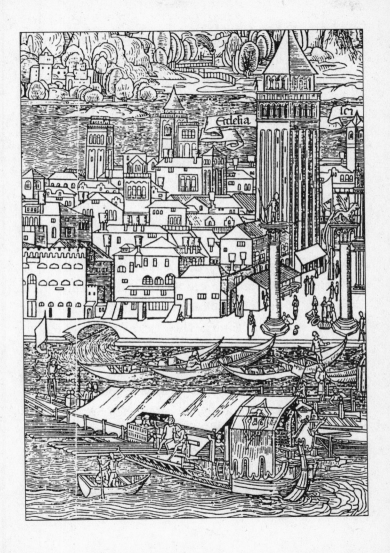

cially in the sixteenth century, when the numerous Christian and Muslim freebooters of the Mediterranean were joined by the powerful warships of northern Europe.

The beginnings of global trading networks

The aggressive approaches of the Hanseatic League and the Venetians to seaborne commerce were to some extent models for the ways that European states dealt with the new trading opportunities opened up by the voyages of discovery made at the end of the fifteenth century by Christopher Columbus (1451–1506), Vasco da Gama (1460–1524) and their compatriots (see Map A, p. x and Map B, p. xii).

Portuguese seafarers forced their way into the maritime commerce of the Indian Ocean region and the Far East in the early sixteenth century. They lacked the resources to completely overwhelm the established networks and their attempts to seize major trading ports and create a royal monopoly on vital trade items such as pepper met considerable resistance. Gradually, however, they became more co-operative than combative in their dealings with Muslim and other non-Christian peoples. They preferred to gain an initial advantage through the use or threat of their naval power and then to tax cargoes passing through the ports they occupied, or to deal out licences to operate within areas that they dominated. Where such tactics could not work, they competed with existing seafarers to carry spices, textiles, ceramics, metals and many other items between the major trading ports and beyond to the markets of Europe and the New World colonies.

The Spanish exploration, conquest and settlement of the Americas were markedly different to the Portuguese penetration of the Indian Ocean region because they opened up completely new forms of long-distance maritime trade. The Spanish extracted massive amounts of silver from the Americas, which not only had a disruptive effect on existing trading relationships across the world, but was also central to the foundation of new extensive trading networks. The Potosí mining complex in Peru was producing more silver than the rest of the world put together by the middle of the sixteenth century. Silver from Peru was carried northwards to Acapulco on the western coast of Mexico and then transferred on to the galleons bound for Manila in the Philippines. Here it was exchanged for a variety of Far Eastern goods, but most especially Chinese silks. These were taken back across the Pacific, by the same galleons, and either disposed of locally or shipped on to Peru and across the isthmus to the Caribbean and eventually back to Spain.

ABOVE: This unfortunate incident occurred at Barry Docks in South Wales in 1908. The steamship *Walküre* had left Archangel in northern Russia bound for Port Natal, with a cargo of timber on her decks. The loading of coal on to her turret deck at Barry caused the ship to list so badly that she was partially flooded. She was pumped out and carried on with her voyage. By the early twentieth century merchant vessels were routinely carrying all kinds of goods and commodities on voyages of thousands of miles.

The Spanish and Portuguese enterprises also moved large numbers of people across the seas to the New World. Some were ambitious colonial immigrants, but huge numbers of slaves were purchased and shipped across the

Atlantic to Brazil and the Caribbean to produce the sugar, tobacco and other commodities that the colonial settlements exported to Europe, Africa and the East.

The arduous, but profitable, trading networks created across the world by the European colonial powers generated an impressive economic momentum, with consequent profound social and political changes. There were many factors involved in the rise of the modern nation states, the spread of modern capitalism and global industrialization, but we can say with certainty that the world economy of the twenty-first century, with all its advantages and problems, has many of its roots in the expanding maritime world of the sixteenth and seventeenth centuries.

III

EMPIRES

We saw in chapter II how strong the urge to trade across the seas has been in human societies since at least the second millennium BC, and how closely the growth of urban communities and powerful states is connected to economic and political networks, both terrestrial and maritime. In this chapter we shall see that there was a major change in the late fifteenth and early sixteenth centuries, when, as a result of the European voyages of discovery, a sudden, dramatic expansion in trading networks occurred, accompanied by the creation of the overseas empires of European nations. For the first time in the history of human civilization societies were able to project their naval and mercantile power beyond long-established boundaries to dominate and exploit new regions. This development laid many of the foundations of the world-wide empires and the global sea-faring trade network of the modern era.

Ancient maritime empires

The ancient Mediterranean world saw the rise and fall of several naval powers. Although the Athenians succeeded in restricting the naval activity of the Achaemenid Persian Empire for much of the fifth century BC, it would be a gross exaggeration to claim that they controlled the sea routes of the eastern Mediterranean, or even of the Aegean, where most of their tributary states were located. Athenian commercial domination was also far from comprehensive.

Early agreements between the two great seafaring powers of the western Mediterranean, Rome and Carthage, are characterized by a spirit of co-operation and respect for each other's spheres of influence. This changed to commercial and political rivalry and developed into a series of wars in the third and second centuries BC. Yet Rome and Carthage do not appear to have systematically prevented each other's maritime trade from functioning. Their traders participated in maritime economic networks outside the confines of the Mediterranean, particularly to the north, where the peoples of the Atlantic coasts had extensive seafaring networks that went back at least as far as

ABOVE: This photo of the reconstructed Classical Athenian trireme *Olympias* clearly shows the three levels of oars on the port side and the bronze ram which was the ship's main weapon. Naval warfare in galleys like this was only feasible in the relatively calm waters of the Mediterranean. Substantial concentrations of manpower (up to 170 oarsmen, plus thirty other crewmen) were needed to make such warships effective. In the fifth century BC the Classical Athenians depended on fleets of ships like this one to project their political power overseas.

the Bronze Age. The Carthaginians also seem to have been interested in opening up trading links with sub-Saharan Africa, but the furthest their explorers seem to have got was the coast of Sierra Leone, reached by the Carthaginian captain Hanno in the late fifth century BC. They did not establish long-term seaborne commerce with the peoples of West Africa (see Map A, p. x).

The Romans were forced to become a sea power by their rivalry with Carthage and they mounted many maritime expeditions against the other states of the Mediterranean and adjacent regions. They even invaded the remote island of Britain in 55–54 BC and again, more decisively, in AD 43. Gradually, over the period from 264 BC to AD 70 the Roman Empire established control of all the shores of the Mediterranean Sea, eliminating all potential competitors. Latin writers liked to refer to the Mediterranean as 'our sea' (*mare nostrum*). It was a busy commercial highway, as we have seen, and it furnished an excellent means of communicating quickly between the imperial authorities and many of the provinces of the extensive Roman Empire. A permanent navy of around 200 ships based in harbours around the Mediterranean was used to maintain this position. There were also some limited extra-Mediterranean naval forces, but the extent of Rome's political power was exceeded by that of the economic networks in which Roman traders were involved. We saw, for example in chapter II, that the seafarers of the Indian Ocean region had considerable connections with the Mediterranean in Roman times, but the Romans did not attempt to extend their political power into this region.

We have already looked at the rise of two European medieval maritime powers, the Hanseatic League and the Venetian Republic, but they cannot be said to have extended their political or commercial influence beyond a stable regional trade network. The same is true of the various Muslim caliphates and empires, which certainly conquered vast areas, but never projected their power overseas to any distant regions or territories which were not already within the sphere of their trading networks. The travels of the celebrated Moroccan geographer Ibn Battuta in the first half of the fourteenth century illustrate this very clearly (see Map A, p. x). Around 1325 he was able to travel from North Africa to Mughal India mostly by land and always within the political networks of the Muslim states. From the Gulf of Cambay he sailed south to Sri Lanka and then north and east to China. He went far beyond regions owing allegiance to any Muslim rulers, but he still remained within the extensive trading network of the medieval Muslim seafarers.

Scandinavian expansion overseas
It could be argued that the raiding, plundering and settlement of France, Britain, Ireland, Iceland and Greenland, as

well as the Swedish incursions into the eastern Baltic and Russia, amount to the earliest manifestation of northern European maritime power being projected beyond an established trading network. The geography of Scandinavia, both on its Baltic and its western coastlines, encouraged communication by sea. Its mountains and forests also drove the inhabitants to make their settlements on lakesides, along rivers and, most famously, at the heads of the Norwegian fjords. From the middle of the eighth century to the end of the eleventh there was a sustained expansion of the Scandinavian peoples across the North Sea, the Baltic and the North Atlantic.

The famous long ships of the Viking raiders were very sturdy, could carry substantial loads of people, goods and animals and were very adaptable. The Norse mariners were comfortable staying at sea for many days at a time, or cruising along uncharted coastlines and exploring navigable inlets and rivers. Swedish warrior and trader bands crossed the Baltic and penetrated deep into the heart of western Russia along the rivers to Novgorod and even Kiev, seeking to control the riverine routes to and from the Baltic and the Black Sea and the territories around them. It was these ventures that brought the people who came to be known as the Varangians into contact with the Eastern Roman Empire of

Constantinople in the tenth century. The naval mobility of the Norsemen gave them the strategic advantage of long range and choice of where to attack, as well as the tactical advantage of surprise when they made their raids. The impact of these raids on their victims was terrifying and disruptive, but it can be seen that where local leadership was strong enough to organize resistance the Norsemen turned away or chose to settle into more harmonious co-existence.

The principle of coming to an accommodation with these seaborne invaders was taken to its logical limit when they were absorbed into the existing political frameworks of England, Ireland, Francia and Russia. Danish Vikings raided and settled in England in the ninth and tenth centuries, creating the Danelaw in northern and eastern England. They were paid a placatory form of tribute, the infamous Danegeld, or absorbed into the English political structure and christianized, although their economic and cultural impact was considerable. Ironically, among the most successful of the Danish Vikings was Knut the Great (1016–35), who, in spite of his joint rule of England and Denmark in the eleventh century, is still best known for his fabled attempt to command the waves. Swedish warrior chieftains established themselves as the rulers of Novgorod and Kiev in the second half of the ninth century. In 911 the Duchy of Normandy was created as a result of the defeat near Chartres of the Viking band of Rolf Gangr by the Carolingian king Charles the Simple. Rolf and his followers had raided north-eastern France for several years. He was persuaded to accept Christianity and baptized as Rollo. Henceforth it was part of Rollo's duty as vassal of the king to keep the Frankish territories of the Seine valley free of other Norsemen. The dukes of Normandy became so powerful that they achieved effective independence in the eleventh century. In 1066, in the wake of the attempt of the Norwegian king Harald III Hardrada to conquer England, Duke William embarked on the most spectacularly successful of all northern seaborne expeditions – the invasion and conquest of England. Another Norman kingdom was created by Roger de Hauteville in Sicily at the end of the eleventh century. Norman rule endured there well into the thirteenth century.

The stimuli for the Scandinavian ventures overseas are varied and none can be readily invoked as a prime cause. A cultural and social disposition towards honouring and praising successful plunderers clearly encouraged the initial Viking raids. The Norse sagas have a certain similarity with the Homeric poems in the way that they glorify violent, seafaring raiders. A great Viking leader could increase his power and status through his choice of suitable targets for raids and the distribution of plunder to his followers. The consequences of successful raiding, and extensive maritime trading, included a more sophisticated and effective leadership in Norway, Sweden and Denmark which adapted its goals to suit the potential of the places visited. Population growth and pressure for land may be part of the explanation for the expansion, particularly among those originating from Norway. The Orkney and Shetland Islands offered only limited scope for plunder and trade, but were suitable for long-term settlement by a small migrant population. Ireland, England and Francia, on the other hand, were prosperous and ideally suited to warriors who could turn themselves into rulers, farmers and, of course, merchants. We should not pass over the fact that many of the seafarers were keen traders. In the Baltic and in the western seas their favoured ports became havens of commercial exchange, like the Viking foundation of Dublin. Political and social changes in Scandinavia also seem to have prompted many to leave. Iceland was settled in the period *c.*870–930 by families and clans who clearly wished to continue to live in the relatively loose structure of hereditary chieftains and their dependants. Emigration to Iceland was mainly from the south-west of Norway, where the centralizing authority of King Harald I Fairhair (870–945) was most strongly resisted, and where many of the Viking expeditions of the previous century had originated. The resurgence of local authorities against the Viking raiders in England, France, Ireland and even Lithuania in the latter part of the ninth century may have encouraged colonization of more distant lands. The relative harshness of life in Norway may also have spurred desperate men to take drastic steps to change their circumstances. Greenland was colonized in the tenth century by a group originating from Norway and Iceland. Its leader, Erik the Red, was a violent man whose homicidal record had made him notorious even by Scandinavian standards. He was following up the accidental sighting of land by a mariner called Gunnbjörn, who had been sailing from Norway to Iceland and was blown off course and decided that this *Groenland* (green land) had at least as much potential as Iceland. Later generations would find that maintaining their preferred forms of civilization in the northern extremes of the world was too difficult.

The families who settled in Iceland and Greenland in the late ninth and early tenth centuries evolved a fairly simple way of life based on the farming of sheep and cattle, on hunting and fishing. The Icelanders did not entirely forgo their Viking traditions, raiding Ireland and Britain in ships that were built from imported timbers. By the end of the tenth century the now Christian population numbered in excess of 60,000, but it depended heavily on Norwegian (and later Hanseatic) traders for imports of timber and grain. Although it could boast rare white falcons as well as their hides, rough woollen cloth and fish products, it is a prime example of an island community that was kept going only through maritime contacts. At the end of the four-teenth century declining Norwegian trade, volcanic activ-ity, a worsening climate and political indifference from the now centralized Scandinavian kingdoms almost reduced Iceland to the same fate as Greenland. Ironically it was English fishing vessels, seeking new areas to ply their trade, that revived the maritime contacts of the Icelanders.

The Greenlanders accepted Norwegian sovereignty in 1261, but their capacity to survive in the face of the deterio-rating climatic conditions, and the accompanying advance of Eskimos from Canada, was dependent on regular seaborne contacts with Norway. As the Norwegians' sea power and maritime trade declined, due partly to the rise of the Hanseatic League and the Baltic states, so interest in the sea route to Greenland dwindled. There was little to be gained from trading with this isolated and desolate place. It produced inferior cloth, a few furs and ivory, but to carry on with the way of life that their society was used to the inhabitants needed such basic materials as grain, timber and metals to be brought across the North Atlantic. In 1370 the one ship to make any regular trips to the eastern settlement at Gardar was lost and there are no records of any contacts thereafter, although adventurous fishermen, or those blown badly off course, may have put in occasionally. A dwindling Scandinavian population seems to have held on until the end of the fifteenth century, but, just as the southern Europeans were about to open up vast new empires in the Americas, the Norsemen's great Arctic adventure came to an end.

The celebrated Norse discovery of North America, an accidental event like the first visit to Greenland, can be easily misunderstood if it is simply viewed as a precursor to Columbus' discovery of the islands in the Caribbean. The essential difference between the two is that the Vikings who travelled to North America had much the same intentions as those who first ventured to Greenland and Iceland. They were looking primarily for lands to settle rather than people with whom they could trade. The famous expedition of Leif Erikson, which sailed from Greenland *c.*AD1000 and explored some of the coastline of Labrador (Markland), as well as Newfoundland (Vinland), spent only a winter and spring there, but his brother Thorvald's group stayed for a couple of years (*c.*1003–5), before being driven off by native Americans. A subsequent attempt to colonize by Karlsefni, a relative by marriage of the Eriksons, involved a substantial cohort of men, women and livestock. They attempted to trade with the native people, but could not establish a *modus vivendi* with them, or even with each other, and so withdrew after a few years.

It is tempting to put these episodes of colonization and conquest in terms of an extensive Nordic maritime empire, but there was no great political, economic or even cultural unity to the territories occupied by the Scandinavians. Trading links and alliances were maintained to some extent, but they were far from exclusive and as time went on they were subsumed in the wider network of interactions between the peoples of Europe. In most cases the Norsemen were absorbed into the societies they encountered. Whether they were Celtic, Anglo-Saxon, Frankish, Hellenic or Slavic they all accommodated the Viking elements. While several enterprising Scandinavian leaders and monarchs managed to become rulers of overseas territories none created a lasting empire. Even Knut the Great's joint kingdom of England and Denmark did not survive his death. Most of the Norse explorations and settlements were individual or family initiatives, involving established leaders and members of ruling families, but they cannot be labelled state enterprises, as was the case with the later European overseas expansions.

China

The political and economic efforts of two dynasties, the Sui (581–617) and the T'ang (618–907), laid the basis for an imperial expansion which resulted in Sung China (960–1279) emerging as the dominant power in the Far East on both land and sea. Chinese naval power was not primarily directed towards the high seas, however, and the expansion of commercial contacts was largely in the hands of enterprising private traders, who often had to contend with an imperial authority that was extremely wary of foreign contacts. To a large extent this can be blamed on the persistent problem of invasions from the steppes.

In the reign of the early Ming emperor Yung-le (1403–24), when China was recovering from the internal disruption and economic problems of Mongol rule, there was a brief period of maritime imperialism, exemplified by the voyages of Cheng Ho (1371–1433). Cheng Ho was a Muslim from southern China who was entrusted with a series of expeditions that were a combination of military

LEFT: This picture of a medieval Chinese war junk distorts many of the key features to give a dramatic effect, but it does illustrate the multiple decks, the highly responsive rigging and steering systems, including a stern rudder controlled by a tiller and a lateral auxiliary steering oar.

and diplomatic missions, intended to assert the prestige and power of China in the Indian Ocean and South-east Asia. They involved some 200 large vessels crewed by nearly 30,000 men – sailors, soldiers, diplomats, scholars and traders. The impact of these voyages was dramatic. Chinese naval power was demonstrated at a time when piracy, particularly from Japan, was a growing problem. China's economic position in the region was enhanced and the imperial court was inundated with rich gifts, embassies from distant peoples, all anxious to better their trading prospects. Yet the successors of Yung-le did not follow up his initiative and attempt to push the boundaries of political power outwards to the fringes of the commercial networks that China was linked into. Instead, again in response to the enormous pressure of incursions on their northern frontiers, they reverted to the defensive, inward-looking posture on both land and sea that had characterized earlier dynasties. External seafarers were still welcome at Chinese ports and there were many Chinese who traded overseas and settled in South-east Asia and India.

The Spanish in the Americas

In 1492 the ships of the Genoese-born master mariner Christopher Columbus (Cristóbal Colón, 1451–1506), sailing westwards from Iberia in search of a route to China and the Indies, made landfall in the Caribbean islands. This most famous of all sea voyages was backed by the Spanish crown and it opened up a new region of the world for the Spanish and other Europeans to exploit.

Spanish settlement of the newly discovered 'Indies' was swift and expanded rapidly. The initial assumption was that the mainland of China lay not far to the west. Once this theory had been shown to be mistaken by the discovery of the coast of central and southern America the Spanish readily grasped the opportunity to settle, conquer, trade

ABOVE: A Chinese naval paddleboat of the twelfth century, propelled by muscle power rather than steam. This kind of vessel was for use on the inland waterways and lakes of China. The attention of the Chinese authorities was generally directed towards maintaining the vast internal economic and military networks. The concept of the paddleboat was known in the Roman Empire, but it was impractical for general use in the Mediterranean.

and exploit the territories on the mainland. It must be stressed that there was a strong determination to profit from the discovery of the Americas on the part of both the royal authorities in Spain and the representatives who came with royal commissions to the New World. The economic enterprise displayed by the Spanish was remarkable. They invested some of the profits of the early conquest of Mexico and Panama into the expeditions to Peru, and the business-men who had backed Pizarro were quick to come to his aid with supplies and men when he was threatened with a major Inca uprising in 1536.

The two most important areas of Spanish conquest were Mexico and Peru. The islands of Hispaniola and Cuba were the staging posts for penetration of the mainland in the first half of the sixteenth century. Panama on the Pacific coast was founded in 1519, the same year that Hernan Cortés took his small army inland from the Gulf of Mexico in search of the gold of the Aztecs. They took full advantage of the political rivalries which already existed within the Aztecs' tributary empire. Cortés and his would-be Con-quistadors had muskets, cannons and crossbows, but he could not have accomplished his remarkable conquest without the assistance of the Tlaxcala state to the east of Lake Texcoco, through which he passed en route to Tenochtitlán and where he retreated in 1520 after his initial attempt to capture the Aztec capital. Furthermore, small-pox, one of several diseases which European settlers intro-duced to the Americas, ravaged first Hispaniola in 1518, then Mexico in 1520. It later spread south to Peru and played a significant part in the ease of the Spanish conquests.

The empire of the Incas in Peru and Chile was defeated by determined Spanish maritime expeditions, led by ambitious and ruthless men including Francisco Pizarro and Diego de Almagro. Ships enabled them to get into a good position to penetrate the Inca Empire and they made good use of firearms and cavalry. They also benefited from considerable internal political strife, following the death of the respected Inca Wayna Capac, from smallpox in 1528. After his death there was uncertainty over which of his sons should succeed him. The civil war between two of them, Huascar and the eventual successor Atahuallpa, provided the Spanish with an excellent opportunity to exploit the political weakness of their enemies. Nevertheless, the conquest of the Inca Empire was a slow affair, complicated by a fierce and deadly quarrel among the leading Conquistadors. It was not really completed until the last centre of active resistance was overcome in 1572.

An important decision was reached in 1494 when the Treaty of Tordesillas between Spain and Portugal effectively established that only the eastern part of Brazil was open to Portuguese settlement. Yet there was no immediate rush to exploit the new lands. It was only in response to the threat of French colonization in Brazil in the 1530s that the Portuguese began to settle and exploit the territory which the treaty had allocated to them. Olinda, the capital of the Portuguese Pernambuco province, was founded in 1535, but by 1600 its port at Recife had become the major urban centre in the area. Bahia, the Portuguese administrative capital of Brazil, was founded in 1549.

There were plenty of adventurous and ambitious emigrants from Portugal and elsewhere who were prepared to cross the Atlantic for the prospect of large land grants and the rewards of the sugar and tobacco trades. Emigrants from Spain and from the Caribbean were also attracted by the scope for commandeering and exploiting the mining and agricultural resources. They imposed themselves upon the native population in its own urban centres and gradually transformed them into versions of the cities of Europe. By no means all those who travelled to the Americas became rich and powerful, for the inequalities of wealth and status that were commonplace in the Old World were magnified by the vast rewards obtained from plundering the new continent. Yet the poorest white peasants were still better off than the indigenous population. The natives, and later the imported Negro slaves, were organized by the settlers and their royal administrators into a labour force that was geared towards sustaining the colonialists and extracting mineral resources or farming cash crops such as sugar and tobacco for export. While there are some similarities between the tribute-paying confederacies of the Aztec and Inca civilizations and the colonial administrations of the Spanish, the social and economic system which developed after the conquest was essentially one in which a tiny European elite held and ruthlessly exercised power over a far larger unfree native and immigrant population approaching 20 million. Gradually the demands for tribute labourers, who were often worked to death, were replaced by a system of wages and contracts, although the terms set by the Spanish lords and masters were harsh and often exceeded. The native population rapidly declined, ravaged by disease, starvation, overwork and cruelty, but its numbers were supplemented by slaves imported from Africa and also from the Portuguese possessions in Brazil.

The Portuguese in the Indian Ocean

Scholars have traced the origins of Portuguese maritime expansion back into the thirteenth and fourteenth centuries, setting it in the context of the progressive decline of Muslim dominance in the Iberian peninsula and the increasing vulnerability of the Moroccan coastline. Italian and Catalan mariners venturing beyond the Straits of Gibraltar had established a considerable knowledge of the north-western coastline of Africa by 1400. In 1415 the Portuguese captured the Moroccan port of Ceuta, just inside the Straits. This success was followed up by the establishment of several coastal trading posts in Moroccan territory, inaugurating a long Portuguese association with Africa. Morocco was part of the wider Muslim world of the Mediterranean, however, and the interference of the Portuguese in the lucrative gold and slave trades eventually provoked a concerted drive to remove them from North Africa. Success was not achieved until the middle of the sixteenth century, and by then other areas had captivated the economic and political attention of the kingdom of Portugal. Inspired by the ambitions of King John I (1385–1433) and his son, Henry 'the Navigator', whose political aims coincided with the commercial desires of merchants keen to disrupt Muslim trade and get direct access to the gold- and slave-producing areas of sub-Saharan Africa, the Portuguese made exploratory voyages to the Azores, the Cape Verde Islands, Madeira and the West African coast.

By the end of the fifteenth century there were several Portuguese trading stations on the Atlantic islands and the west coast of Africa, of which the most important was at Elmina on the Gulf of Guinea. The Portuguese established this fortified base in 1481. It provided slaves and, in particular, gold from the African states and tribes in exchange for a variety of European goods, including textiles. Towards the end of the sixteenth century the emphasis shifted away from gold to (male) slaves, who were shipped across the Atlantic to the Caribbean and to Brazil. The island of São Tomé, discovered in 1473, was developed into an early example of the 'colonial factory' method of production, using slave labour to cultivate sugar and operate refining mills. Slave revolts were common in these areas, and the relatively sophisticated economic and political structures in many of the African kingdoms which the Portuguese encountered enabled them to resist attempts at Portuguese domination. There were also other Europeans interested in the same areas. The Spanish were making trading voyages to the coast of Benin by the 1470s, but in the sixteenth and seventeenth centuries it was the Dutch who gained the most from Portugal's African possessions. These developments encouraged the Portuguese monarch John II (1481–95) to seek opportunities further south and, it was hoped, east. King John directed his mariners to explore further around the coast of Africa and they responded by going as far as the extreme south of Africa and the margins of the Indian Ocean. Bartolomeu Dias in 1487–8 explored the coastline to the Great Fish River and returned only when his crews became mutinous. He named the headland he passed on his way back to the Atlantic the Cape of Good Hope, because it offered the prospect of discovering the route to the Indies. In the face of considerable opposition in Portugal, which was grappling with its neighbour Spain over the division of the newly discovered territories to the west, the new king, Manuel I (1495–1521), launched the expedition of Vasco da Gama, to find Christian monarchs in the east and put Portugal at the centre of the trade with the Orient (see Map A, p. x).

Vasco da Gama's royally commissioned voyage of exploration received a mixed welcome on the East African coast. He came into conflict with the authorities in Mozambique and was forced to leave Mombasa without the pilot he needed to help him reach India. His arrival at Malindi was well timed, however, as the local ruler saw in the Portuguese potential allies against his hostile neighbours. From there Da Gama set sail across the Indian Ocean under the guidance of an experienced Indian Ocean navigator, Ibn Majid. In Calicut the Portuguese ships were afforded a cordial welcome. Da Gama had letters of introduction from his king to the ruler, and he obtained a substantial cargo of spices, even though he lacked much in the way of goods to trade for them. Da Gama was by nature much more of a soldier than a diplomat and there were some tense moments before his ships were allowed to depart. On the whole the impression which this expedition left on the predominantly Muslim seafaring communities of the region was an unfavourable one. Their fears were confirmed over the following few years, as it quickly became clear how aggressive and acquisitive the European traders were. They took control of a series of ports from the east coast of Africa to the west coast of India. They occupied Mombasa in 1505 and made it a key base for their military and commercial ventures, although the port was never easy to control and there were repeated attempts to remove the occupying forces.

The Portuguese crown officially created an organization called *Estado da Índia* (Indian State) in 1505 to provide the political framework for the dramatic entry of the Portuguese into the Indian Ocean region. The corresponding commercial organization, the Indian House (*Casa da Índia*), was principally aimed at dominating the lucrative spice trade, particularly the trade in pepper, which accounted for almost three quarters of the commerce in spices by the sixteenth century. The principal pepper-producing area was the Malabar coast of India. The early Portuguese enterprises involved attempts to cut off the long-established Red Sea route, operated mainly by Muslim seafarers, and thereby to deprive the merchants of Catalonia, Venice, Alexandria and the Levant of a major source of supplies. In their place a Portuguese royal trading monopoly was envisaged, directed by the *Casa da Índia*. For this purpose the port of Aden at the entrance to the Red Sea was attacked in 1513, but it resisted doggedly, and the whole endeavour was eventually thwarted by the Ottoman Empire's determined if costly protection of the old routes. A later expedition forced its way right through to the Gulf of Suez, but the Portuguese naval forces were not sufficient to take on such a large territorial empire. The Portuguese were, however, successful in their conquest and domination of some of the vital entrepôts in the region. They occupied a series of key ports including Cochin in 1503, Goa in 1510 and Hormuz in 1515. The Portuguese in Goa took over the business of supplying Asian horses to the Hindu Vijayanagara elite in southern India from the Sultanate of Honovar. They maintained reasonable relations with the Vijayanagara to ensure the profitability of their trade against competition from the Muslim ports of the Malabar coast to the south, several of which had small naval forces.

The main advantages the Portuguese possessed in the early sixteenth century were their superior naval equipment and techniques. These were founded on sturdy, ocean-going vessels with heavy cannons in their armament and aggressive raiding tactics. The Portuguese were largely ignorant of the politics and diplomatic intricacies of the regions they had launched themselves into, but they did their best to divide and conquer. Resistance to the European interlopers was briefly co-ordinated in Gujarat by a 'League of all the Muslims'. Its combined fleet was not an organized navy, however, and it was comprehensively beaten in a battle at Diu on the Gulf of Cambay in 1509. The Sultan of Gujarat's governor in Diu then came to terms with the victors. Several other ports under Muslim and Hindu control followed suit, forced into allowing the Portuguese to extract revenue from tolls, harbour duties and protection money for the guarantee of escort or non-interference by Portuguese vessels. Refusal to co-operate meant laying harbours and merchants open to plundering by the same ships. Cochin allied with the Portuguese against Calicut, its rival to the north, and Calicut was forced into line in 1513. In contrast with many of their victims the Portuguese had the advantage of a fairly consistent and coherent political purpose, with the resources of the crown behind the major enterprises of the *Estado da Índia.*

While they were successful in establishing several dominant positions on the western coastline of India, on the eastern seaboard the Portuguese could not overcome the power of the Muslim merchant communities of Goloconda and the Carnatic states. Nor could they make serious inroads into the South-east Asian trade carried by the mariners of Masulipatnam, which became the principal port of the Mughal Deccan. The Mughal Empire was firmly established in India in the mid sixteenth century. Its principal creator was Akbar, grandson of the first Mughal ruler Babur. Akbar was not Indian himself, but his policy of marriage alliances with the Rajput princes produced a dynasty that identified closely with both the Muslim and the Hindu cultures of India. Mughal power grew steadily under Akbar's ambitious descendants and by the end of the seventeenth century much of India was under direct or indirect Mughal control, although the rise of the Hindu Maratha Confederacy in southern and central India presented a serious challenge, which led to the dissolution of Mughal power and the rise of a host of semi-independent principalities around the southern and eastern seaboards and along the Ganges valley. Later European initiatives were to expose and exploit the limitations of Mughal power.

An early aim of the *Estado da Índia* was to proceed beyond the subcontinent to the spice islands and other fabulously wealthy lands that were said to lie to the east. The earliest Portuguese voyage to Malacca was in 1508, but it was only in 1511 that Portuguese royal forces led by the ruthless Afonso de Albuquerque captured this vital port in the extensive spice trade network of the Indian Ocean region. Its Muslim rulers were forced into exile, founding the Sultanate of Johore on the southern tip of the Malay peninsula as a political and commercial rival to Malacca.

Imperial and commercial rivalry with Portugal's neighbour Spain lent a certain degree of urgency to the investigation of the possibilities in South-east Asia. The small clove-growing islands of Ternate and Tidore were embroiled in a war which submerged their local quarrels under the weight of Iberian conflict. The Spanish retreat in 1529 gave the Portuguese a virtually free hand, which they used heavily, provoking considerable resentment. For fifty years Ternate was little more than a fortified warehouse for the collection and shipment of Moluccan cloves, mace and nutmeg. Expansion to Tidore, Amboina and Banda Islands was carried out with the local Muslim rulers' approval, but the increasingly unpopular Portuguese were driven out of Ternate by the same rulers in 1575.

Arguably the greatest Portuguese economic impact was in the Far East. Chinese authorities considered driving the Portuguese out of Malacca, which they viewed as a territory within their sphere of influence. The first Portuguese visit to the Canton river occurred in 1516 and initial trading ventures to southern China were both profitable and peaceful. Attempts to construct yet another fortified base and establish a Portuguese monopoly on maritime trade were rebuffed by Chinese naval forces and imperial officials, leading in 1521 to an official Chinese ban on trade with the Portuguese. This prohibition was, however, regularly broken by commercially ambitious traders from both sides, who met in small ports or on tiny islands away from bureaucratic eyes. There was a change in the official attitude to Chinese merchants trading overseas from the mid sixteenth century. Limited commercial interaction was officially allowed from 1567. High seas ship building in China had not been particularly buoyant under the influence of the imperial ban. Thus foreign seafarers had a distinct advantage. The Portuguese restarted direct trade with China from their small island base of Macao in the Pearl River estuary, established in 1557. They imported ivory, ebony and Peruvian silver, via Malacca and exported silks, ceramics and Chinese copper, mercury and camphor. Silver coinage had been introduced in China in the fifteenth century and supplies of Japanese silver were readily supplemented by the Spanish bullion from the New World. The Spanish themselves traded with China through Manila from 1571 onwards. They brought in silver from Mexico and Peru and took away silks, spices and ceramics.

Portuguese discovery of the route to Japan did not occur until 1542–3, when an expedition heading for China was accidentally driven there by a typhoon. The Japanese proved very accommodating and Macao to Nagasaki became a lucrative trade route for Portuguese ships carrying Chinese goods. After the loss of Malacca to the Dutch in 1641 the merchants of Macao shifted their business more towards the Philippines, supplying Chinese silks to the Spanish, whose powerful galleons then exported it to Acapulco in Mexico.

The Portuguese cannot be dismissed as simply imperialists, motivated by greed for riches and greater trade; some also mixed a religious zeal in with their commercial instincts. For some the desire to dominate trade in the Indian Ocean region was mixed with anti-Muslim feelings and rivalry with fellow Christians. Albuquerque and Pedro Álvares Cabral are examples of the aggressive imperialists who desired a substantial Portuguese maritime empire, operating its trading monopolies under a centralized authority. On the other hand there were merchant venturers who opposed the violent imperialists and who were able to invoke an already well established royal law that permitted Portuguese to trade on equal terms with non-Christians, rather than attempt to conquer them and take control of their networks by force.

Modern scholars have argued that, for all their energy and ambition, the Portuguese did not totally disrupt the dynamics of trade in the Indian Ocean region. They became major figures in maritime commerce, but they were far from achieving total dominance and eventually faded under pressure from both local resistance and competition, and the arrival of strong European competitors. Eventually they settled into a more co-operative participation in the maritime trading networks of the region as partners, albeit rather violent and unpredictable ones.

The dream of a royal monopoly on oriental trading was never realized and the *Estado da Índia* regularly granted licences and concessions to private merchants. This practice gradually undermined the revenues of the crown from the eastern trade and encouraged a host of other European mariners to enter the region, initially in partnership with Portuguese merchants, but soon in competition and

conflict with them. Chinese and Japanese mariners benefited from Portuguese willingness to share technical expertise in order to increase commercial traffic. In the long run
the Portuguese lacked the manpower and economic resources to overwhelm their competitors. They were also
distracted by the development of the Americas and Africa,
and by contests with European rivals and non-European
powers who formed alliances against them. For example,
the pepper-producing city of Achin (Atjeh) in northern
Sumatra was regularly visited by European shipping, but
its excellently positioned harbour, a centre for trade in
spices and gold, was not occupied, despite the efforts of
French, Dutch and English forces. Achin's maritime
traders regularly carried their own merchandise directly to
the Red Sea ports, avoiding the Portuguese vessels pa-
trolling the more northerly routes to India and the Persian
Gulf. The city assisted Malacca in driving out the Portuguese in 1641. The rise of the Ottoman Empire
(c.1450–1921) in Turkey and the Near East, and the Safavid
Empire (1501–1722) in Persia were concurrent with the development of Portuguese interests in the Indian Ocean
region. There is more to this than mere coincidence. The
two great Muslim powers controlled important areas of
the hinterlands of the Persian Gulf and Red Sea and they

limited the scope for the Portuguese, or any other Europeans, to dominate the trade networks in these areas. The Portuguese were driven out of Hormuz in 1622 by Shah Abbas (1587–1629) and his fleet of English allies. They were finally expelled from Mombasa in 1698 by the naval forces of the Imam of Oman.

Dutch and English East India Companies

The English, French and Dutch initially obtained African, Asian and American products via the thriving Atlantic ports of Cadiz and Lisbon. In the sixteenth century, as a consequence of the religious and political conflicts produced in Europe by the Protestant Reformation and the Catholic Counter-Reformation, they were frequently banned from these ports and denied access to their highly lucrative cargoes. Their exclusion from the growing transoceanic trade encouraged them to turn to piracy and privateering (state-sponsored piracy) and to attempt to establish their own trading links with the Indian Ocean and American regions. Adventurous seamen such as Francis Drake and Walter Raleigh led expeditions on behalf of private companies of merchants, who pooled resources to finance and equip raiding and trading voyages to the Americas and to the east. The arrival of these marine adventurers changed the nature of European interaction with the civilizations of the East. Their combination of merchant vessel and warship became a respected and feared sight in eastern waters.

In 1602 in the Dutch republic a company called the *Vereenigde Oostindische Companie* (United East India Company, hereafter VOC), was formed to exploit the opportunities offered in the East Indies. Ironically it was partly thanks to their long struggle with the Spanish monarchy that the Dutch developed a strong merchant fleet. At the start of the seventeenth century the Netherlands was a major trading partner of France, Spain and Portugal, supplying food, cloth, raw materials and a host of manufactured items, including weapons. The Dutch were very good high seas mariners who were used to operating large-capacity cargo ships, carrying commodities such as wine, cloth, timber and salt in the waters of the Baltic Sea, North Sea and the Atlantic Ocean. The British East India Company (EIC) was established in London in 1600. It had smaller resources and fewer ships than its Dutch counterpart, but, like the VOC, it used an auction system to maximize profits and diversify from spices into textiles and tea. EIC ships were faster, allowing their captains to keep to tighter timetables. They also tended to be much better armed than Dutch vessels.

ABOVE: This unusual Chinese painting of the eighteenth century shows a European trading ship (possibly an East Indiaman) at anchor, awaiting the loading of its cargo of porcelain and the reloading of its cannons. The guns of the European ships were greatly feared by Far Eastern states that lacked similar artillery or suitable defences against them. Many of the distinctive features of northern European ships are expertly illustrated here, especially the large and varied array of masts and sails.

From the outset the approach of the VOC to the Indian Ocean trading networks was very aggressive. The Dutch allied themselves with Portugal's rivals, such as the cities of Johore and Candy, to drive the Portuguese out of Malacca and Ceylon. They also preyed on places with weak local rulers, such as on Java where they established their main South-east Asian base at Jakarta (renamed Batavia). Both companies used naval bases to concentrate their resources for easier operations. They ranged far across the region bringing strategically important ports under their control. A great deal of the resources of the VOC were concentrated on South-east Asia and the Far East to secure a dominant position in the growing trade with China and Japan. They gradually moved from dominating trade to dominating production centres in the seventeenth century, especially the pepper and spice production areas in Ceylon, Malabar and the Moluccas. The English had bases in Bombay, Madras and Calcutta and operated a great deal in the Arabian Sea.

The Dutch and the English were initially allies but soon split as the English were excluded from the spice trade and driven out of some of their territorial bases. Rivalry turned to conflict as the almost incessant European wars of the seventeenth and eighteenth centuries realigned the major maritime powers, with the English turning to the Spanish and Portuguese as allies, and the Dutch to the French. It was in this period that the cohesion of the ancient trading networks of the Indian Ocean region was seriously ruptured. Inevitably the European nations' political and commercial interests became closely interwoven in these conflicts. Gradually British military and naval strength, both in Europe and across the world, enabled the EIC and other colonial agencies to bring more and more regions into an extensive maritime empire.

Britain's maritime empire

Many British families are, quite reasonably, proud of their ancestors' achievements in the Indian subcontinent, but there is an alternative perspective which can be adopted on the way that India gratified the appetites of the British Empire. For example, British-led changes in demands for Indian textiles in the eighteenth century had a dramatic effect on Bengal. Pressure from home textile workers had forced a ban on imports of printed cotton. Thus the British switched their requirements to white cloth, which could then be most easily obtained from Bengal and shipped to Britain for further processing. The result was a huge increase in British cotton trade with Bengal, carried in British ships, of course, and close British involvement in the economy and politics of Bengal. The long-term economic effect of this was, however, to make the Bengalis heavily dependent on the income they gained by weaving cotton for export. When the production and shipping advances triggered by the Industrial Revolution enabled British cotton products to dominate, the industry in Bengal collapsed and they were forced to return to agriculture. The unrest in Bengal had a political effect, strengthening the position of the Nawab of Bengal against the Great Mughal, but it also drew the EIC into Bengal as an independent military force. Clive of India's successes led, in 1756, to the EIC taking over the administration of Bengal and the collection of taxes. These revenues helped the EIC to finance later territorial conquests in India and also to buy tea in China, taking silver away from India's economy.

The EIC might have organized India as a commodity-producing state, but for the Industrial Revolution, which was partly aided by the influx of wealth from India into private merchant capitalist hands, but which was largely driven by the extensive trading network that the British had established in the eighteenth century. This network provided the markets for exports to boost the production which otherwise would have been much smaller if it had

concentrated on a home market. The EIC therefore replaced the feudal rulers such as the Great Mughal and the
Nawabs, but transferred abroad much more of the tribute
from the agrarian, artisan and merchant population. The
efficiency of the naval and army forces used by the EIC, plus
the high quality of their generals, enabled them to overcome the resistance of the Indian rulers and other European powers, particularly France, whose forces were
expelled from southern India in 1761. A vital aspect of the
exploitation of India was the British merchant marine.
Britain's mariners took the manpower and expertise to
conquer and administer out to India, then they carried the
profits of India back home. As the Industrial Revolution
worked its changes on the productive capacity and financial
scope of Britain, India and other imperial possessions furnished a market for the goods they needed to sell and the
ships of the EIC and others ensured that they could be
transported there.

The EIC introduced a more contractual approach to the
extraction of revenue from India's peasants. This is seen in
the Permanent Settlement of Bengal of 1793, which defined
the peasants as tenants of the government, whose rent was
a fixed contractual sum, rather than a variable tax. Through
this mechanism the EIC began to remove much of the silver

that had come into India. The overall effect of increasing British rule was a depression of the Indian economy in the early nineteenth century. The historian Dietmar Rother-mund has summarized the relationship between Britain and India thus: 'The East India Company as a modern capitalist corporation of an advanced bourgeois nation entrenched itself like a parasite in the agrarian state dominated by a decaying military feudal regime.'[1] In 1813 the EIC's monopoly on trade was removed and the company ceased to be a trading company at all after 1833, selling its indigo and silk businesses and concentrating on administering its slice of empire. It is a sad fact that Indian exports to Britain and China were in considerable surplus for the early part of the nineteenth century, but the EIC was forced to remit large amounts of money to London, so there was no commensurate growth in the Indian economy.

Another example of the British exploitation of their overseas empire is furnished by the case of the Indian railways. Whilst British transport historians can claim that the way that India's railways were built and equipped by British companies is a tribute to British engineering and entrepreneurship, historians of India's economy might argue that they are a testament to the greed and self-interest which characterized the administration of Britain's overseas empire. Railways were being constructed in the 1850s at an impressive rate. Industrialization was slow, however, and even the 1858 institution of direct rule over India did not end the parasitical nature of the British occupation. Political unification of India, pursued by Lord Dalhousie, a railway expansionist in Britain, did make the development of transport systems easier. By 1900 there were 25,000 miles of track. Yet, although in 1865 the Indian railway locomotive construction industry started, it was far cheaper to import engines and rails from Britain. Hence in the period 1865–1941 only 700 locomotives were built in India, but 12,000 were imported from Britain, encouraged by the easy passage offered by the Suez Canal, opened in 1869. Furthermore, the capital invested from Britain in this construction was at an attractive interest rate of 5 per cent, which was paid for by taxes on Indian taxpayers. Well into the twentieth century Indian nationalists criticized the British for putting money into railways rather than irrigation programmes, which would have been more beneficial to the largely agrarian population. One could argue, nevertheless, that the British in the second half of the nineteenth century and the early twentieth century were laying the foundations for their own destruction. The incorporation of India into a British legal framework required the schooling of many

Indian lawyers, one of whom was Mahatma Gandhi. The railways carried the people who became politically active from one place to another and they allowed the circulation of newspapers, which were essential to the growth of national consciousness and political awareness. The relationship between Britain and India in the period *c.*1750 to 1947 can be fairly characterized in terms of a parasitical maritime empire. The British conquered India through a marine trading company (the EIC) and they then exploited it from afar, relying heavily on their naval and merchant marine resources to facilitate this exploitation. The Indian Ocean and other formerly separate regions were caught in a political and economic power network so extensive that it encompassed virtually the entire globe. Whatever crises occurred within this network affected all parts, producing world wars and global economic depressions.

IV

RELIGIONS

The sea and seafaring can be said to have many close connections with religious beliefs and practices. Ships and boats have been used in many religions to symbolize journeys to the afterlife and fish are also symbols of death and the afterlife. Small models and even full-size ships are often discovered by archaeologists in the context of votive offerings, burials and other forms of religious rituals. Seafarers as a distinct group have certainly never been irreligious people. There is arguably no better way to confront the limitations of human power than by venturing out to sea (see Illustration on cover). The celebrated Jesuit missionary Francis Xavier was moved to make the following remarks after completing a voyage from Lisbon to Goa in 1542:

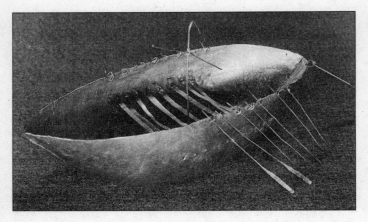

ABOVE: This exquisite gold model of a small vessel with a mast and oars was found at Broighter in Ireland. It is dated to the first century BC. Ships have been used as religious offerings by many civilizations. They range in size from tiny models like this one to full-size craft used in processions and burials.

During our voyage we heard the confession of many who were sick and of many others who were well. I preached on Sundays. Praised be the Lord for having been pleased to grant us the great peace that, while we were sailing through the fishes' realm, we found people to whom we manifested his word, and to whom we administered the sacrament of penance, which is no less necessary on the sea than on land.[1]

In this chapter we will examine the relationship between

seafaring and the spread of some of the world's most important religions. Once again the sudden expansion of European maritime networks which occurred in the sixteenth century will be seen to have profound effects, this time in terms of religious as well as economic and social interactions between civilizations.

Buddhism

Its founder was Gautama, the Buddha ('Enlightened One'), who was born *c.*560 BC in northern India, on the border with modern Nepal. After marrying and having a son he experienced a series of encounters which changed his perspective on life and led him to seek spiritual enlightenment through asceticism and meditation. Although he was the son of an aristocrat and had a relatively high social position in the Hindu caste system of the time, he rejected some of the most important social and philosophical tenets of his own culture and established a mendicant order. He spent his later life teaching his new principles of the elimination of desire and anguish through the pursuit of ultimate enlightenment (Nirvana). He died in *c.*486 BC, but his teachings were spread widely in South Asia and the Far East. Male and female monastic orders formed the core of the Buddhist faithful.

Buddhism was in many respects a sect that developed in the context of Hindu religious and social beliefs. Hinduism is a term which covers potentially all the religions of the people of India. As a collection of religious beliefs and practices it embraces both internal meditation and elaborate external ceremonies, as well as the extremes of asceticism and carnal indulgence, vegetarianism and (in the past) cannibalism. It also accommodates a large pantheon of deities and other beings with divine associations, about whom an impressive corpus of sacred texts (the Vedas), featuring mythical tales and wisdom literature, has been developed. Not surprisingly for such a complex range of cultural and spiritual codes, there was no significant missionary element to Hinduism. Buddhism was originally a reforming movement within Hinduism, and its early converts were among the peoples of northern India. Although the most famous of these was Asoka, the ruler of the Mauryan Empire (274–232 BC), whose conversion resulted in a significant change in the nature of his rule, its spread was not dependent upon political developments. Rather it was carried along trade routes, both terrestrial and maritime, to other parts of South Asia and the Far East. Eventually Hinduism adapted itself to the needs of an increasingly diverse society, adopting some crucial aspects of Buddhist philosophy.

Buddhism largely disappeared from India in the eleventh and twelfth centuries AD, partly as a result of the Muslim conquests and partly in response to the revival of Hinduism. Followers of the Buddhist way also adopted aspects of the pantheistic approach to religious authorities characteristic of Hinduism.

Buddhism was well established in Ceylon by the third century BC. The majority Sinhalese population, particularly the ruling classes, provided the main source of adherents. Their patronage, including measures such as the remittance of taxes on lands donated to the monasteries, helped to sustain Buddhism in the face of pressure from the Chola Empire's occupation of Ceylon (AD 1017–70), as well as the powerful Portuguese and Dutch maritime incursions of the sixteenth and seventeenth centuries. Chinese Buddhism dates back to at least the first century AD, although its transmission was clearly via terrestrial contacts in central and South-east Asia. From there it spread to Korea in the fourth and fifth centuries AD. Korean missionaries introduced Buddhism to Japan in the 520s, where the acceptance of a combination of the Buddha's laws and the way of the gods (Shinto) was proclaimed by the Soga emperor Jomei in 587 and promoted by his prince regent, Umayado (573–621). The Ritsuryo rulers of the seventh and eighth centuries were particularly enthusiastic in their advocacy of Buddhism at all levels of society. It was embraced by the Japanese elite as a way of providing a measure of religious legitimization for their social status. In the nineteenth century Chinese and Japanese immigrants carried Buddhism to Hawaii and their missions established it in the United States of America. Europe has also received Buddhist missionaries from South Asia, principally in the United Kingdom, which at the start of the twentieth century had very strong maritime connections with Ceylon.

Perhaps the most important aspect of Buddhism was its emphasis on an individual's capacity to achieve self-enlightenment and (ultimately) spiritual salvation. It could be argued that its appeal to growing urban communities, and especially to those used to regular maritime travel between communities, was due in part to its capacity for adaptation to changing social structures, in contrast to the more hierarchical aspects of social control and conformity which characterized (early) Hinduism. It could also be seen as a more attractive system of beliefs for the enterprising, socially mobile merchant than many local religions, not just Hinduism, which assigned merchants to a relatively lowly position in their socio-religious hierarchies. There can be no doubt that Asoka's example was widely followed among the mercantile communities of the region, but they were not the only ones to do so. The adoption of Buddhism by the ruler of a major state was bound to encourage further converts with a wide range of motives, as we have seen in the case of Japan.

While it is tempting to link the spread of Buddhism to the continued growth of long distance maritime trade in South and South-east Asia, there is no simple cause-and-effect relationship involved. Buddhism was probably more of a response to social and economic change than a creator of them. In the South Asian civilizations of the late first millennium BC and the early first millennium AD, the growth of Buddhist monastic centres may well have encouraged the accumulation of wealth among artisans and merchants by providing them with the opportunity to present some of their profits to monasteries as pious donations. Donations to monasteries by individuals from a very wide range of occupations are a feature of Buddhism from its earliest historical phase and many Buddhist monastic sites are found in or near the trading ports of the western and eastern Deccan in India. These sites were to some extent furnishing a new forum for displays of enhanced prestige and social status before the regular gatherings of fellow Buddhists. This trend was repeated in other parts of Asia.

From the maritime perspective a particularly interesting development of early Buddhism was the evolution of a protective patron of seafarers, along with other travellers, called the Bodhisattva. The cult of this manifestation of the Buddha, who has the power to save sailors from the monsters of the sea or from the dangers consequent upon being shipwrecked, is adumbrated in several texts of the third and fourth centuries AD. Sculptural representations and a variety of other references to the capacity of Buddhist seafaring merchants to invoke spiritual protectors suggest that Buddhism might have been perceived as especially attractive to adventurous mariners. Nevertheless, it is clear that seafaring played only a limited role in the spread of Buddhism, and that the way of the Buddha was never overwhelmingly attractive to merchants or mariners in the regions where Buddhism was established. Buddhism was never contiguous with a particular trading network, nor was it expanded beyond the confines of the maritime networks in which Buddhist social groups participated.

Christian maritime missionaries
The connections between Christianity and seafaring are as

ancient as the Christian faith itself. The Gospels make it clear that fishermen from the inland sea of Galilee were among Christ's earliest followers. We may speculate that he was drawn to them because of their marginal social and economic position, which was typical of all fishermen within the Roman Empire, but he does not seem particularly to have sought or attracted adherents elsewhere among the seafarers of Palestine. Nevertheless the spread of early Christianity has a notable maritime element, featuring the recruitment of fishermen, the symbolic use of fish and fishing and other marine connections. The missionary journeys of St Paul (d. *c.*AD 65) were facilitated by the ease of sea travel within the Roman Empire in the first century AD, although even the Apostle of the Gentiles was not spared from the perils of the sea, being shipwrecked on Malta whilst travelling to Rome for his trial. It can also be argued that maritime communications within the Roman Empire were an important feature in maintaining the unity of the Christians, both before and after the conversion of the Emperor Constantine (AD 306–37). The main centres of Christianity outside the immediate environs of Palestine and Syria were mostly clustered around the maritime trading ports such as Alexandria, Cyrene, Leptis Magna, Carthage, Massilia and Rome. Seaborne travel between them was commonplace and quick. The Christian communities were able to communicate with each other across the length and breadth of the Empire about such matters as doctrine, relationships with the state authorities and social and pastoral concerns. As it spread out beyond the confines of the Roman world Christianity maintained its beneficial relationship with the sea. The Christian patron saint of sailors and merchants, St Nicholas, was the bishop of the Lycian coastal trading city of Myra (Mugla in southern Turkey) in the fourth century AD (see Illustration on cover).

The ancient Atlantic maritime trading (and raiding) networks feature strongly in the history of Christianity in Britain. Perhaps the most famous example involves the early adventures of St Patrick (*c.*390–460), who was captured at the age of sixteen by Irish pirates, who presumably took him back to Ireland. He was apparently kept as a slave for six years before managing to gain his freedom and returning, presumably in a merchant ship, to his home on the west coast of Britain. He returned to Ireland as a missionary bishop around 435 and won his reputation for conversion of pagans in the northern regions. In this sense he was continuing the work begun in the southern part of the island by St Palladius, an emissary of Pope Celestine I (422–32), who later crossed over to Scotland. The legends and stories surrounding the life of St Illtyd, a fifth-century abbot of the monastery at Llanilltydd Fawr (Llantwit Major) in Glamorgan, mention him sailing to Brittany with several merchant ships carrying grain to relieve a local famine. The maritime missionary aspect of Christianity was to reassert itself strongly in western Europe from the end of the sixth century AD. Pope Gregory the Great (590–604) sent the famous mission of St Augustine of Canterbury (d. 604) to Kent in AD 596, but it was the Celtic Church in Ireland that made the greatest progress in the task of converting the heathen Anglo-Saxons and Franks. The relative isolation that its position on the edge of the Atlantic gave to Ireland had largely preserved its Christian communities. Led by outstanding figures such as Columba (*c.*521–97) and Columbanus (*c.*543–615) the Irish crossed the sea to Scotland, Wales and France. From monastic strongholds such as Iona, Lindisfarne, Caldy Island and Luxeuil the missionaries gradually brought about the conversion of most of the English and Frankish kingdoms in the seventh century AD. There were also expeditions in the opposite direction from the Roman Church in Gaul to southern England. The links between Britain and the mainland of Europe allowed Englishmen such as Willibrord (658–739), Boniface (680–754) and Alcuin (735–804) to play leading roles in the life of the Frankish Church.

The conversion of Scandinavia provides further examples of the importance of maritime trade networks in the spread of Christianity. One of the early missionary bases for Christians seeking to bring their message to the heathen Norsemen was the joint bishopric of Bremen and Hamburg, whence the Frankish missionary bishop St Anksar (801–65) regularly ventured to Denmark and Sweden, whose respective kings, Björn and Harald Klak, were well disposed towards Christianity. Anksar concentrated his attentions on thriving coastal market towns such as Birka in Sweden and Hedeby and Ribe in Denmark, where the relatively cosmopolitan merchant communities were more receptive to Christianity, and where churches were established that became the foundations for later expansion. Their success was mixed, partly due to the differing attitudes of the various pagan Scandinavian kings, who were mindful of the strong reactions of some of their subjects to the monotheistic Christian message.

A somewhat different aspect of maritime communications had a significant part to play in the evangelizing efforts of the Norwegian king Oláf Tryggvason (995–1000). Not content with using the example of his own conversion to Christianity to encourage his people to follow suit, Oláf sent several missionaries to Iceland at the end of the tenth century to persuade the Icelanders to accept the Christian faith. When the latest of these, a rather aggressive Flemish priest called Thangbrandr, returned to Norway without having had much success, King Oláf took several important Icelanders hostage and threatened to kill them unless Christianity was accepted on the self-governing island. While they might consider themselves to belong to a free state which acknowledged no king's direct authority, the Icelanders recognized that Norway was their main trading partner, and that, as we have seen in chapter III, they were heavily reliant on the regular visits of Norwegian ships for their prosperity. Within a couple of years not only had the majority of important families converted, but official pagan rituals were abolished.

In the east it was largely the activities of the Nestorians from Persia which were responsible for the appearance of Christian communities in South and South-east Asia and China. Muslim authorities did little to hinder the spread of Christianity, at least until the age of the Crusades, when intolerance became a problem for both Christendom and Islam. The presence of many Nestorian Christians among the seagoing merchants of the Indian Ocean undoubtedly helped to promote the spread of their religion. The St Thomas Church in India, with its strongholds on the western coast, was effectively an offshoot of the Nestorian Church. The Nestorians even managed to establish themselves in China in the period of the T'ang dynasty (618–907), moving eastwards along the central Asian trade routes from Persia. Although there were Christian churches in the seventh and eighth centuries, the hostility of Buddhists and the prohibition on all 'foreign' religions in the middle of the ninth century finally caused the extinction of Christianity in China.

Under the rule of the Mongols China was targeted by Christian missionaries sent by the thirteenth and fourteenth century popes who had hopes of converting the Mongols and gaining their alliance against Islam. One such missionary, a Franciscan called Giovanni di Monte Corvino (1247–1328), followed the ancient maritime trade route from Hormuz to the east in 1297, arriving at the court of the new khan, Timor, in 1299. Corvino and his entourage received a friendly welcome and his initial successes led to his being created Bishop of Beijing (Khanbalijk) in 1307. The papal registers of Clement V (1305–14) show that he was assigned 'the care of all the souls in those parts that are subject to the lord of the Tartars'. He did apparently convert around 6,000 Mongols and added a second cathedral in Quanzhou to his own in Beijing. Yet Corvino's bishopric did not last beyond his death, nor did his congregations survive the collapse of Mongol power in 1368. Indeed, the later Jesuit missionaries to China were not even aware of the efforts of their Franciscan predecessors. It does not seem unreasonable to assign part of the blame for the failure of the medieval missionaries to the lack of a direct maritime link between China and Christendom. Without the support of a trading network that carried a strong Christian identity, enabling regular contacts with other Christians, the small communities in Mongol China were bound to struggle to maintain themselves.

The isolated circumstances in which Giovanni di Monte Corvino was trying to operate were a strong contrast to the situation which prevailed when the Jesuits, led by men such as Francis Xavier and Matteo Ricci, began to establish their Far Eastern missions in the sixteenth century. St Francisco de Jassu y Xavier (1506–52) was one of the six priests who founded the Society of Jesus in 1534, under the leadership of St Ignatius of Loyola (1491–1556). Francis Xavier was assigned to the missions in the Far East in 1541, at a time when, as we have seen in the previous chapter, Portuguese and Spanish trade and settlement within the region were increasing. He sailed on the first stage of his journey from Lisbon to Goa on a ship with the Portuguese governor of Mozambique, and was able to move quite freely around the coasts and islands of South and South-east Asia. After several years' work in southern India, Ceylon, the Moluccas and Japan he embarked on a journey to China, but died on an island off the Chinese coast whilst awaiting official permission to enter China. Matteo Ricci (1552–1610) was successful in penetrating China at Kwangtung in 1583, moving via Nanking to Beijing in 1601. He arrived at a time when relations between the Ming Chinese authorities and the Portuguese were strained, but the possibility of sophisticated cultural exchange had been established after several decades of commercial interaction. Furthermore, there were Portuguese and Spanish colonies and missions at several locations within easy reach. These acted as something of a support and communication network. Christianity remained a minority religion in China, but by the end of the eighteenth century the members of that minority numbered around a quarter of a million.

Islam

The Prophet Mohammed died in AD 632. Within ten years the Arabs had overrun most of the Persian Empire, and were making substantial inroads into the territory of the Byzantine Empire. Within a few centuries Muslim traders and seafarers dominated the maritime commerce of the Arabian Sea, the Red Sea and most of the Indian Ocean. They reached as far east as southern China and the margins of the Pacific Ocean. It is one of the small ironies of the spectacular growth of Islam that the ruling merchants of Mecca were originally hostile to the new prophet and his growing band of followers, in part because they feared that they might threaten the continued importance of their sacred shrine, the Ka'ba, and Mecca's position as the commercial centre of western Arabia. Their eventual acceptance of Mohammed and his message paved the way for him to transform Mecca into one of the greatest pilgrimage destinations in the world, a status which enhanced its commercial importance as well. Seaborne pilgrims flocked to the holy city in ever increasing numbers and from ever greater distances in the centuries following Mohammed's revelations. Each year the pilgrims embarked upon the *hajj* in their tens of thousands, representing a vast movement of buyers, sellers and their goods, drawing many other traders with them. This annual gathering, as predictable as the monsoon winds themselves, boosted the commercial and cultural importance of Mecca and Medina. Even today the

ABOVE: This illustration from a thirteenth-century Muslim manuscript (the *Maquamat* of al-Harari) shows several of the features of Muslim craft of the Indian Ocean region, including the stern rudder, an iron anchor and twin masts, one of which has an observation platform. The passengers may be representative of pilgrims making the *hajj*.

hajj is a highly significant element in the economy of Saudi Arabia, although many of the pilgrims travel by air, coming as they do from all corners of the global world of Islam.

Under the leadership of Mohammed himself the Muslims conquered western Arabia and Oman, gaining control of major ports on the Red Sea, the Gulf of Aden and the Straits of Hormuz. The Prophet's immediate successors, Abu Bakr, Omar and Othman, extended Muslim control to both sides of the Persian Gulf and parts of the south-east Mediterranean. Over the course of the following 800 years Islam spread as far west as the Atlantic coastline of Iberia and Africa, and as far east as the Moluccas and the Philippines. Expansion along the East African coast began in the eighth century and by 1050 Muslim merchants were heavily involved in exporting the products of the hinterland to Arabia, the Red Sea and South Asia. They displaced the Christian merchants of Aksum, to the detriment of that kingdom and its port of Adulis. The spread of Islam along the African coastline proceeded at a similar pace and in a similar fashion to that through the islands of South-east Asia. The two regions were also brought closer together in economic terms. Ports such as Malindi and Mombasa developed into urban centres with stone mosques. They were ruled by merchant dynasties deriving partly from the

Middle East and South Asia, but predominantly native to Africa. They exported cowrie shells, ivory, slaves and, from the thirteenth century onwards, gold. There was some regular commercial contact with the agricultural states of the interior, such as Zimbawe, from where gold was transported to the port of Sofala on the Mozambique coast, but Muslim cultural influence in these areas was minimal. The inhospitable terrain and the prevalence of diseases in the interior discouraged the coastal settlers from moving inland.

In many cases the conversion of South-east Asia to Islam began with the establishment of small communities of Muslim traders. Thus Muslim seafarers from the Middle East settled in the vibrant, cosmopolitan ports on the western coast of India, the east coast of Africa, the Malay peninsula and the islands of Sumatra, Borneo and Java. They intermarried with the local population and achieved considerable independence in the conduct of their affairs. There can be no doubt that it was this ability to appeal to all groups in society that enabled Islam to take root among communities where the influx of wealth from maritime trade led to loosening of the traditional hierarchical social order. Gradually the Muslim way of life also penetrated the hinterlands, but in both East Africa and South-east Asia the absence of cosmopolitan trading communities inland meant that there was less potential for the spread of the religion. In some cases conversion to Islam in South-east Asia was achieved under the patronage of the Sultanate of Malacca. The established hierarchies and cultures of the islands of South-east Asia were replaced by a political and social order which was both more favourable to the aspirations of the merchant communities and, because it was drawn towards the Islamic centres of the Middle East and South Asia, more easily integrated with these areas economically. By the end of the fifteenth century Malacca was one of the great trading ports of the world.

Islamic authorities encouraged agriculture, manufacturing and trade in the great Islamic Empire(s) (*Dar al-Islam*) which grew up in the wake of the Muslim conquests. Political and economic stability were promoters of commerce as they had always been. Both Muslim and non-Muslim merchants prospered. There were, for example, numerous communities of Jews across the Muslim world. We are well informed about the situation of the eleventh and twelfth century Jews in Egypt and elsewhere, thanks to the famous documents of the Cairo *Genizah*. The vast range of records surviving from this community offers us revealing glimpses into a world of seafaring merchants who were at the heart of a prosperous commercial network extending from western Europe to India.

The political dimension to the spread of Islam should not be underestimated, of course, as it was principally through the military success of the armies of the caliphates that the *Dar al-Islam* was enlarged. Nevertheless, the political limits of Muslim power were always narrower than the economic and religious boundaries of Islam. The conquest of Sind in the eighth century AD, for example, brought the Indus delta under Muslim control, but it was not until the eleventh century AD, under the impact of Turkish invasions, that the northern half of the Indian sub-continent began to fall under the sway of a series of Turkish and Afghan sultanates. Even at the height of its power in the fourteenth century AD, the Delhi Sultanate was only able to make intermittent taxation and tribute demands on the southern provinces. Political unity has long been as impossible a dream for the Islamic world as for the Christian.

The first Christians in the Americas

The religious aspect of European maritime expansion to the Americas is a difficult one to evaluate. There can be no doubt that the overseas expansion of the fifteenth and sixteenth centuries had strong overtones of an extension of Christendom. It was the officially declared policy of the Spanish crown, for example, that the conversion of native populations to Christianity should have the highest priority. Yet, as we have seen in the previous chapter, there were other priorities at work in the conquest of the Americas that had nothing to do with Christianity. Nevertheless, there can be no doubting the strength of the belief of many of the Conquistadors that they were doing God's work and that his power was what was allowing them to succeed, often against seemingly overwhelming odds. The promotion of Christianity was certainly a major part of the interplay between the leading Conquistadors and the rulers of the Aztecs and the Incas. Cortés' first landfall in Yucatán in 1519 was marked by the destruction of pagan idols and the erection of a Christian altar to celebrate mass. When Montezuma took him into the shrine of the war god Huitzilopochtli in Tenochtitlán he asked for permission to erect a Christian altar there and demanded that an image of the Virgin Mary be placed on top of the great pyramid temple. Disputes over religious issues certainly played some part in the breakdown in relations between the Spanish and the Aztecs.

There is also a clear missionary element to the accounts

of Pizarro's initial contacts with the Incas. In his first exchange with the Inca governor of the outlying town of Tumbes in 1528 Pizarro insisted that he and his small expedition had come to persuade the Incas to abandon the worship of false gods and become Christians. This approach was repeated when Pizarro and his followers finally met the great Inca Atahuallpa at Cuzco in 1532. Unfortunately the first sign of reluctance to accept Christianity was not met with understanding and kindness, as the official policies enjoined, but with intolerance and violence. The priest who had accompanied Pizarro's expedition, Friar Vicente Valverde, is singled out by most of the accounts as the instigator of a massacre when Atahuallpa rejected his peremptory command to abandon his own gods. Later expeditions, such as those of Orellana and Cabeza de Vaca, were characterized by a genuine desire to understand the indigenous culture and religious beliefs, and to demonstrate to them the superiority of Christian ways, but the general tenor of early Spanish and Portuguese treatment of the indigenous peoples of Central and South America was intolerant and oppressive. By the time genuine missionaries began to catch up with the Conquistadors in the middle of the sixteenth century the damage had already been done. They faced a harder struggle trying to rescue the bodies of the native populations from their European masters than to save their souls from pagan ways.

North American settlements

The pattern of European penetration and colonization of North America was very uneven. The coastline of the Gulf of Mexico was explored by the Spanish in the mid sixteenth century, and in the wake of some of the maritime expeditions adventurous and ambitious explorers penetrated some way inland. The first permanent European settlement on the North American mainland was founded at St Augustine in Florida in 1565. By the beginning of the seventeenth century Spanish vessels had even reached the coast of Alaska. The sophisticated tribal cultures of the northern native peoples helped to make their resistance to Spanish encroachment strong and at times well co-ordinated. Colonization and agricultural exploitation were accompanied and often led by evangelization. The papal designation of the majority of the New World as a Spanish domain contained an inherent expectation of the spread of (Catholic) Christianity among its indigenous inhabitants. To begin with, the maritime mobility of the Europeans made it easier to establish and build up settlements on the coastal areas. In the seventeenth and eighteenth centuries chains of mission stations were established in New Mexico, Texas and along the Pacific coast from Baja California northwards. The gradual penetration of the interior of the West, still attested by the names of such states as Montana and Nevada, laid substantial foundations which were built upon by later generations of settlers. Competition for the Spanish came from the French and the British, whose interests in North America grew steadily during the seventeenth and eighteenth centuries.

In the first half of the sixteenth century French mariners were very active in the Caribbean and the Atlantic, as rivals of their Iberian neighbours, spurred on by the religious and political conflicts in western Europe. They had a fearsome reputation for their raids on shipping, capturing numerous vessels returning from Brazil and Mexico, and on coastal settlements, the most spectacular of which was an attack in 1555 on Havana, in which Royal French naval vessels participated. A Franco-Spanish peace treaty of 1559 acknowledged Spanish control of Central and South America, but left the question of European claims to the northern territories open.

Religious wars were fought with great ferocity in France from 1562 to 1598, when the Edict of Nantes created a political framework for the co-existence of Catholics with the

Protestant minority. There were further outbreaks of hostilities in the 1620s, and in 1685 King Louis XIV revoked the Edict of Nantes, forcing many Protestants to flee abroad. The ports on the English Channel and the Atlantic coast of France were places where the Calvinist Protestants found many adherents. The harbour towns of Dieppe, St Malo, St Nazaire and La Rochelle had long traditions of trading with both the friends and the enemies of the French monarchy. The maritime skills and prosperity of the seafaring communities in such places, especially La Rochelle, were matched by a strong sense of independence from the authority and policies of the Paris-based Catholic rulers in the sixteenth century. Piracy and privateering became major contributors to their economies, and to that of the mainly Catholic Bretons in the sixteenth century.

There can be no doubt that religious conflicts in France played a major part in the early attempts at overseas settlements. The Huguenots were quick to realize the possibilities inherent in establishing colonies which could provide sanctuary for the reformed Christians and trading revenues for the hard-pressed Protestant cause at home, and act as naval bases for assaults on Catholic interests in the New World. The Protestant leader Coligny sponsored the Chevallier de Villegaignon's ambitious project to settle a mixed Catholic and Protestant community on one of the small islands in the Bay of Rio de Janeiro. After five years of quarrelling and trying to scratch a living in unfamiliar conditions the settlers were driven out by Portuguese forces. Further attempts followed, concentrating on the north-eastern coastline of Brazil, but only one of them, Cayenne, founded in 1604, survived the Portuguese drives to eliminate them. Coligny was also behind Jacques Ribault's attempt to colonize Florida in 1562. This area was ideal for attacking the Spanish silver convoys as they departed the Gulf of Mexico on their way home. It was at Port Royal in South Carolina that Ribault and his motley group of fighting men, women and children first tried to make their settlement. Its failure was followed in 1564 by a small colony at Port Caroline, in the north-eastern coast of Florida. English assistance was provided at a crucial point, as the colonists struggled to make a new way of life work, but the Spanish swiftly intervened to remove these potential threats to their American revenues. An alternative model of creating trading companies to take a share of the lucrative commerce between Europe, the Indies and the Americas was tried with some success by Calvinists based in Normandy, as well as by Catholics from the ports of Brittany, but competition from the Dutch and continued civil strife severely limited their effectiveness. Central and South America were to be settled and exploited almost entirely under the Catholic authorities.

In the north, however, the story was a very different one. We have already noted the brief Scandinavian adventures on the north-western fringes of America. The native population in these areas was small, but its tribal structures were well developed and their territorial coverage fairly comprehensive by the sixteenth century. There was virtually nowhere in what was to become the United States and Canada that European seafarers could expect to make a landfall and avoid contact with the indigenous populations, but the absence of overarching political frameworks meant that the Europeans had to make a very different sort of territorial progress through North America from that achieved in Central and South America.

The English, French and Dutch colonists who sailed to North America in the sixteenth century were unable to take the kind of action that the Spanish had in Central and South America by virtue of the lack of large-scale territorial empires in this region. The native Americans treated the Europeans with a great deal of caution. For example, the long-standing rivalry between the Iroquois and the Huron, who occupied territories to the south and north of the

St Lawrence river, afforded some opportunities for the Europeans to find markets for their weapons and to acquire allies for their own internecine conflicts, but they also helped to ensure that neither the English nor the French found any easy passage into the heart of the North American continent.

The existence of a large landmass with impressive river inlets was known in general to French and British fishermen from the early part of the sixteenth century. They visited the Grand Banks off Newfoundland and the Gulf of St Lawrence to catch whales, walrus and the abundant cod. They also traded with the native population for furs and skins, particularly otter and beaver. It was not, however, the desire to exploit the natural resources of seas and rivers which prompted French and English settlement here. Instead it was the search for the mythical north-west maritime passage to the wealth of Asia that drew English and Spanish maritime expeditions to the region. They charted the outline of the American coast in the 1520s, but found no obvious routes through to the east. John Cabot claimed Newfoundland for the English crown as early as 1497, but significant settlements on the Atlantic seaboard to the south did not begin until the 1620s.

French expansion into Canadian territory was slow

until the seventeenth century. Jacques Cartier, an experienced mariner from St Malo, led several expeditions in the 1530s and 1540s to Newfoundland and into the St Lawrence river, discovering the large Huron settlement at Hochelaga (Montreal) under native guidance. Cartier was supposed to establish colonies with a largely convict population and to ensure that the churches he built were Catholic ones, in spite of the fact that he was a Huguenot. He achieved little of consequence, however, and the religious wars drew attention away from this region. It was in 1603 that another product of the French Atlantic seafaring community, the Catholic convert Samuel de Champlain, realized that the Algonkians and Hurons were engaged in trade with other peoples further inland where there were large rivers and lakes. Champlain was responsible for the founding of the trading post at Quebec and he was instrumental in persuading Cardinal Richelieu to establish a royal trading company, the Company of New France, in 1627. This organization was given a wide territorial remit and charged with settling several thousand French Catholic families on land to be cleared for agriculture. Protestants were forbidden to join the new settlements.

There was considerable enthusiasm in France and in Rome for the prospect of converting the innumerable

Indian souls to the true faith. The challenge of converting the North American masses was primarily taken up by the Jesuits, whose Portuguese and Spanish brethren had established a range of techniques from reasoned to forceful persuasion. The seventeenth-century papacy was, in principle, strongly opposed both to violent conversions and to the enslavement of pagan peoples. The Congregation for the Propagation of the Faith (often called 'the Propaganda') was created in 1622 and among its first acts was the propagation of two fundamental principles for the work of Christian missions, namely the recruitment of indigenous clergy and respect for native customs, which should not be subjected to immediate change.

The Jesuit missionaries tried hard to understand and come to terms with the peoples of North America, but the prospects for success were not good, however, as there was little in the Christian message to attract the Canadian tribes. They practised polygamy, had their own morals and traditional laws to regulate internal and external relations and their view of the spiritual world was incompatible with Christianity. They did not live in large, permanent villages or towns, so it was difficult to gather them into churches. Furthermore, the most desirable items of trade the Europeans could offer them were guns and alcohol, which the

Jesuits themselves could neither readily approve of, nor easily condemn.

Several missionaries were martyred, particularly by the Iroquois, whose conflict with the French and the Hurons, the principal French allies, was sharpened by the introduction of European weapons and by a rivalry over the profitable trade in furs with the Dutch, English and French settlers. French attention turned to the Mississippi river and the vast territory named Louisiana as English interest in the St Lawrence area grew in the seventeenth century. The Hudson Bay Company, founded in 1670 to seek the north-west passage and occupy the area around the bay named after its English discoverer, Henry Hudson, developed as a major competitor in the fur trade. In the eighteenth century the naval powers of France and England fought wars across the globe, inevitably involving the inhabitants of New France and their Huron allies. English military successes in Europe and elsewhere were accompanied by treaty concessions and a rapid decline in French influence in North America. Ultimately, the Christian Europeans brought their own religious and political divisions across the Atlantic Ocean along with their weapons, their alcohol and their deadly illnesses, of which we shall have more to say in the next chapter. From the native Americans' point of view it must often have seemed that the white men brought only decline and death.

English activities in North America were characterized by a strong sense of political and religious rivalry both with the French and, especially in the second half of the sixteenth century, with the Portuguese and Spanish. Protestant ardour at the English court fed off the recent experience of a Catholic monarch whose ruthless suppression of Protestants was encouraged by her Spanish consort. More worldly passions were fuelled by envy of the wealth the Catholic monarchs were extracting from their maritime empire. The English also harboured a growing confidence in the capacity of their ships and seafarers to emulate and even surpass the achievements of their European rivals. To take one famous example, the voyage of Francis Drake that started in 1577 was aimed primarily at undermining Portuguese and Spanish power in the Americas by attacking ships and settlements, contacting native Americans who were known to be resisting further Spanish conquests and scouting possible locations for bases and colonies. Drake's small fleet was financed by both crown and courtiers, who expected to profit materially, as well as politically and diplomatically, from his endeavours. He forcibly obtained a Portuguese pilot in the Cape Verde Islands, worked his way around the coastline of South America and headed north, attacking coastal settlements such as Valparaiso, and even capturing a treasure ship heading for Panama. His landings on the Californian coast were accompanied by extravagant claims of English sovereignty in 'New Albion'. Next, with more reluctant Iberian navigators to guide him, he crossed the Pacific heading for Manila. He negotiated a commercial treaty with the ruler of the spice island of Ternate in 1579, before returning home via the Cape of Good Hope. Drake's circumnavigation was more violent and acquisitive than that of Magellan and del Cano and it provided a foretaste of the maritime imperialism that the English were to embark upon over the course of the following two hundred years. An initial English attempt to establish settlements in North America was made at Roanoke in North Carolina between 1585 and 1590. The colonies founded under the new English king, James I (1603–25), were more successful, helped by the creation of chartered companies to promote settlement in Virginia and Plymouth Bay. By the 1630s there were several thousand settlers in Virginia, mainly growing tobacco for export to England.

The English colonies in North America that were to form the nucleus of the United States had a strong religious character almost from the outset. Many of the early settlers were 'Puritans' whose campaign to enforce a strict, Calvinist ethos within the established English national Church had manifestly failed to achieve its aims by the end of the sixteenth century. Some of the Puritans, grouped into 'gathered churches', were persuaded by their leaders that they needed to separate themselves from the Anglican Church. Initially they went to the Netherlands, but the prospects of creating a more godly, independent religious community in the New World encouraged them to found settlements to the north of the territory controlled by the Virginia company. The most celebrated group of a hundred or so religious colonists were the 'Pilgrim Fathers', whose ship the *Mayflower* sailed from Plymouth in November 1620. They founded a settlement at Plymouth Bay in December. It was a brave undertaking and they were fortunate to survive the voyage, make a safe landfall and to befriend the local native population early on.

More colonies were founded, their numbers swelled by the increasingly disillusioned Puritans, until by 1640 there were some 20,000 settlers, mostly concentrated around Massachusetts Bay, where the United Colonies of New England were born, during the political and religious upheavals of the early 1640s. The devout Protestants were missionaries as well as refugees, converting thousands in the native communities around them and working to translate the scriptures into local languages. Like those of their Catholic counterparts to the north and south, however, their activities were not always peaceful and there were several bloody conflicts in the early stages involving massacres of the indigenous population. New England also became a focus for Christian fundamentalist missionaries, whose views on basic tenets of Calvinist orthodoxy were staunchly opposed. Over time more settlements of Quakers, Anabaptists and other Christian sects were established. To the south of Massachusetts Bay the settlers of Rhode Island were more tolerant, welcoming Baptists, Catholics and Jews into their communities.

The relatively easy seaborne mobility available to the different groups of colonists encouraged them to seek out alternative locations for their settlements along the coastline to the north and south of Cape Cod. In 1632 a colony was founded at Chesapeake Bay in Maryland under the patronage of Cecilius Calvert, Lord Baltimore, whose intention was to furnish a haven for English Catholics, but not to the exclusion of Protestants, who made up roughly half of the colonists. This experiment in overseas religious harmony was short-lived, however, as bitter conflicts developed between the dominant Catholics and some of the

Puritan settlers. In 1689 the Calverts were deposed and the Catholics lost power. In the 1670s large numbers of Quakers settled in the territory of West New Jersey. From there they explored inland, and in 1681 the Quaker leader William Penn used his royal patronage to secure a charter for the foundation of what was to become Pennsylvania. By the end of the seventeenth century there were around 250,000 inhabitants in the British colonies and by the middle of the eighteenth century the combination of high levels of reproduction and floods of new arrivals had pushed the total over the two million mark. The changes in the speed and size of seagoing ships, and the interlinking of maritime commerce into a global economy, which occurred in the nineteenth and twentieth centuries, also facilitated large-scale immigration, from many parts of the world.

Although the American colonies were closely integrated with Britain in both political and economic terms, their inhabitants were multi-national and multi-denominational in their origins. The Dutch and German Reformed Churches provided a substantial proportion of the Protestant settlers, especially after New York was added to the English possessions in 1664. German Lutherans migrated to America in large numbers in the eighteenth century, as did Presbyterians from Scotland and Northern Ireland. Evan-

gelical theology found a fertile breeding ground in eigh-
teenth-century America, where a heady mix of religious
views made reflection on spiritual commitments and the
relative merits and statuses of different congregations and
their ministers something of a commonplace. It is hardly
surprising that religious toleration, freedom of expression
and the rights of local communities to determine their own
policies were, and to a large extent still are, major issues in
the politics of the United States.

V

FOOD AND HEALTH

The relationship between seafaring, food and disease is largely determined by the nature of the trading networks that carry people and commodities across the seas. Significant economic and political developments can be seen to have major implications for the civilizations of the world at the basic level of food and health.

An example of these implications can be taken from a topic that has come up already. The increasing use of the monsoon winds to carry trade goods across the Indian Ocean region, which promoted the traffic in spices from China, South-east and South Asia to Arabia, East Africa, the Near East and the Mediterranean, can be seen to have had an influence on food preparation, and vice versa. Eastern spices became increasingly sought after as ingredients in

Roman cooking from about the first century AD. The famous recipe book of Marcus Gavius Apicius, which is probably a fourth- or fifth-century compilation but is based on an earlier, first-century version, makes extensive use of imported spices, especially pepper. The recipes of Apicius were not, of course, those which the ordinary citizens of the Roman Empire were likely to follow, but they give us a reasonable indication of what demands the rich, prestige-conscious elites might make upon their marketplaces. Once particular items, such as pepper, had become established as necessary luxuries of high-class lifestyles, the demand for them was constant. The continued importance of spices as preservatives, as well as flavourings, ensured that the spice traders could always find a market for their wares among the wealthy elites of the Mediterranean and its neighbouring regions. It can be argued that the increased use of preservatives in food also led to improvements in aspects of storage and the nutritional value of diets. We will now briefly consider some examples of how seafaring developments have been influential in bringing about changes in the staple foods of the diets of historical civilizations, and thereby played a significant part in wider social, political and economic developments.

Fishing

Fishing predates the development of human civilization by a considerable length of time. It is argued by a number of European prehistorians that, because the skeletons of Neanderthals show evidence of a deficiency in vitamin D, otherwise obtained by prolonged exposure to sunlight in latitudes closer to the equator than 40°N, they did not consume fish, which they would probably have had to obtain by the use of specialized equipment unattested from the Neanderthal period. By contrast there is considerable archaeological evidence from later prehistoric human cultures of fishing tools and fish bones. The search for fish would have encouraged ventures out on to the water, beyond wading depth, and so played a major role in the development of seafaring. All historical societies that have had access to the sea have harvested it for food, but fishing, while it was an important supplement to foods produced on land, was rarely the mainstay of a people's diet. As was the case with several other aspects of seafaring, however, there was a marked expansion in the scale and intensity of western European fishing activities from around 1500, leading eventually to the creation of a global fishing industry.

In the sixteenth century the settlement of North America by the British, French and other Europeans was accompanied by a spectacular growth in the fleets which, as we have seen, fished the teeming waters off the coast of Newfoundland, New England and Maine. By the end of the century hundreds of ships were participating in the cod fishing and whale hunting bonanza. A considerable proportion of the fish caught went to feed French, Spanish and Portuguese populations that, partly as a result of the dietary requirements produced by the Catholic Counter Reformation, were becoming more accustomed to eating fish than ever before. Recently improved drying, salting and transportation methods enabled the rich harvest of fish to be sold and distributed throughout western Europe. Whales were hunted for their meat, their bones and their oil. The latter briefly became a staple of the lamplight industry in the nineteenth century. As with so many other aspects of nineteenth century seafaring the whaling industry was dominated by the British, but Scandinavian and American ships were also prominent. Both whaling and fishing had become important industries for many of the world's seafaring nations by the end of the nineteenth century.

The rapid progress in seafaring technology brought huge changes in the nature of the world's fishing fleets in the twentieth century. Large ships, powered by steam and diesel, along with refrigeration techniques, allowed fishermen to travel further from their ports, to stay at sea for longer and to process larger catches. Sonar and other sophisticated detection methods have helped to make fishing a high-tech industry. Larger, more 'efficient' nets that can be trawled by one or more ships at depths of up to 900 feet can catch so many fish that there is growing pressure on governments and international organizations to ban certain types to conserve fish stocks.

The growth in fishing productivity since 1900 was associated with an increased demand. Fish could now be regularly consumed by people who lived far from the sea. In Britain this demand was led by the 'fish and chip' shops, which are now seen as an integral part of the national culture. A less obvious, but highly significant development, was the increased use of fishmeal for fertilizer and animal feed. The rising demand for such products was a major factor in the overfishing of herring and mackerel in the north Atlantic, for example, and it is also threatening the supplies of smaller fish such as anchovies and even krill. A growing international awareness of the overfishing problem in the last twenty-five years has produced zoning of fishing waters, regulation of the gear used to fish and systems of quotas and licences, which have caused many fishermen to abandon the harvest of the seas. National interests have clashed repeatedly over the issue of access to fishing grounds and conservation of stocks. In the 1970s Iceland and the United Kingdom even engaged in some tense naval manoeuvres known as the 'Cod Wars' to protect their fishing rights.

Whaling acquired a romantic image thanks to the famous novel *Moby Dick*, Herman Melville's story of a New England whaling ship and its fanatical captain, but in recent times the history of whaling has come to be viewed as a tragedy for the great whales themselves. In response to overfishing of the northern Atlantic waters some of the whalers headed into the Pacific and the south Atlantic oceans in the early twentieth century, briefly turning the remote island of South Georgia into a centre of the whaling industry. Ultimately the success of new technology spelled the decline of the whaling industry, which could not continue to consume the great whales at such a rate. The rorqual or 'right' whale was hunted to extinction in northern waters, the sperm whale population was drastically reduced in the Pacific and whales in general have become a symbol of the need to conserve the marine environment. Since the early 1990s only Japan has continued to operate a significant whaling industry, mainly to serve the local demand for whale meat.

Rice

Rice was first domesticated in South-east Asia. Its use spread north-west and north-east to China and South Asia in prehistoric times and, in several varieties, it was the staple crop of the peasant farming communities which gradually emerged in India and China. These communities were to form the agricultural basis for some of the early civilizations of the Asian continent. Rice growing was a fundamental part of the economy of the civilizations of eastern Asia. The dramatic growth in the Chinese population between the ninth and twelfth centuries was sustainable only because of improvements in the cultivation of rice. Some were technical, such as the use of better irrigation and cultivation tools and the practice of systematic planting out of seedlings. Biological improvements also occurred, notably the adoption of early ripening varieties of rice from the Champa coast of Vietnam, which were imported into coastal areas in the eleventh century AD and later distributed across the rice farming areas by the Sung government. They enabled peasants to grow a second, winter crop, producing far larger surpluses than before.

One of the great advantages of rice as a cargo is that it does not deteriorate as rapidly as other foodstuffs. It can be kept in storage for several years and used to supplement poor harvests or even to relieve famines in particular areas. The role of rice in the maritime trade of the Indian Ocean region needs to be understood not only as a staple of the diet of many parts of Asia and Africa, but also, because it has long been cultivated in a tremendous number of varieties, as a delicacy. Merchants could make substantial profits by shipping Bengali varieties to Ceylon and the Maldives, or Madagascan rice to the mainland of East Africa.

The rice trade between South-east Asia and China was a large-scale, highly prosperous aspect of the maritime trade of the South China Sea from the eighteenth to the early twentieth centuries. It was entirely in the hands of Chinese and Thai merchants who were able to resist attempts by Europeans to break into it. Rice was, nevertheless, just one of the foodstuffs which western Europe began to import in large quantities from the Indian Ocean region in the nineteenth century to feed its increasingly urban, industrialized populations. The spread of rice as a cash crop was another feature of the maritime trade explosion of the last few centuries. By the end of the nineteenth century rice was being grown extensively in North America, where it is still a major part of the agricultural economy.

Potatoes

Several new staple foods were introduced to the Old World from the New World in the sixteenth century, including maize, manioc, potatoes and several varieties of sweet potatoes and yams. They assisted in the population growth that sustained the massive seaborne transfer of native Africans to the Americas. This transfer of people was itself a response to the demand for a cheap, servile labour force to grow the crops required by European settlers in their new territorial empires. The most famous food of all to have come from the Americas to Europe is the potato. The potato has been credited with improving the nutritional intake of the poorer parts of the population of northern Europe. It was a staple food of the indigenous inhabitants of the upland valleys of Colombia and Ecuador, and was discovered by the Spanish in the late 1530s. Their sailors were consuming it in the mid sixteenth century and it was introduced to Spain in the 1570s. From there it was swiftly disseminated among the countries of Europe. It is Ireland that popular imagination most readily associates with the spread of the potato, however, because of the high degree of dependence upon potatoes among the rural population, which developed during the seventeenth century. The catastrophic outbreak of potato blight in Ireland in 1845 and

1846 produced the infamous potato famine which, with its consequent outbreaks of diseases such as cholera and typhus, reduced the population by around two million.

Sugar and slavery

The sugar cane (*saccharum officinarum*) was probably first domesticated in South-east Asia as early as the seventh millennium BC. It was originally grown in New Guinea and, perhaps, Indonesia, and was carried to India no later than the fifth millennium BC. By the time Alexander the Great's forces reached the Indus valley in 327 BC it was widely used in foods and beverages, combined with milk, barley, rice, ginger and other substances. The earliest written description of a sugar-refining process comes from a Hindu document of about AD 500, a reference that uses the analogy of boiling the juice of the sugar cane to make a kind of molasses that can be rolled into balls. Although it was a widely grown and widely consumed substance in the Indian Ocean region in the first millennium AD, sugar did not reach European trading markets very often and was considered a luxury of Arabia and India. The Muslim conquests of the eighth and ninth centuries were responsible for the introduction of sugar cane growing, which requires careful management of the water supply, into the Mediterranean region, particularly in North Africa and the islands of Cyprus, Rhodes and Sicily. The commercial and administrative expertise fostered by the caliphates was put to good use in developing the infrastructure for sugar growing, refining and distribution. Gradually the Europeans acquired the taste for sucrose and medieval Venice was an important entrepôt for the distribution of sugar to other parts of Europe. The Christian conquests and re-conquests of territories held by the Muslims for centuries provided the 'crusaders' with an important education in the processes of sugar production. The overlords of the Latin East became the supervisors of sugar producing plantations in Cyprus, the Levant and Malta in the eleventh and twelfth centuries. In the fourteenth century the focus of production seems to have shifted from the eastern to the western Mediterranean.

São Tomé, the Canary Islands and Madeira were the early focus of the Portuguese sugar industry. The island of Madeira was colonized by the Portuguese in the early 1420s, as part of the great maritime expansion sponsored by Prince Henry the Navigator. The island is blessed with an agreeable climate and very fertile soil. The main crops grown there in the first hundred years or so of its development were wheat and sugar. Readily available African slaves were used in the cultivation and the labour-intensive production of sugar for export to the rest of Europe. The Mediterranean sugar industry was severely damaged by the success of the Madeirans, although in the latter part of the sixteenth century the growth of a more extensive sugar-producing economy in the Americas, especially Brazil, forced them to turn to other crops, notably wheat and vegetable dyes such as woad. The introduction of vines on to the island led to the production of the sweet wine which is now the best known of all Madeira's exports. Madeira and the more northerly Azores, which were also settled in the 1420s under Henry the Navigator's Atlantic programme, were important stages on the route to and from Iberia and the Americas. São Tomé's significance as a sugar production centre dates to around 1500. When the economies of these places began to be overshadowed by the New World many of their inhabitants joined the migrations to Brazil.

Sugar cane growing was spread by European settlers and colonists to South America and the Caribbean in the sixteenth century. Since then it has become a staple export commodity for Brazil and the West Indies, which ship it all over the world. The early European settlers were unwilling to engage in dishonourable manual labour themselves, nor, indeed, were there sufficient reservoirs of population in Iberia or other parts of Europe to furnish the labour, for they had to be prepared to emigrate to the New World and undertake difficult work, often under harsh conditions, on the plantations. As a result of the decline of the indigenous populations which followed swiftly upon the arrival of the Europeans, large, subservient labour forces were urgently required. They were obtained from the slaving ports of West Africa. The rise of the sugar trade is, therefore, closely connected with the most infamous of all maritime commercial activities, the slave trade. It is clear that slaves had been involved in the sugar industry for a long time, both in the Near East and the Mediterranean, but it was the relatively sudden expansion of sugar growing in the Atlantic that gave a strong impetus to the development of the slave-based sugar plantation.

The first regular shipments of slaves were to Santo Domingo from around 1509, to work in the Spanish-controlled gold mines. In 1515 skilled sugar cane cultivators were brought to the Caribbean from the Canary Islands and the new sugar plantations of Santo Domingo began to export their product to Europe in 1516. Their output was soon overtaken by that of the Portuguese colonies in Brazil and many other locations on the Pacific and Atlantic coasts of Central and South America. The early decades of the Atlantic slave trade were dominated by the Portuguese, whose merchants had an official monopoly on the West African trade routes. In the seventeenth century the British, French and Dutch presence grew swiftly on both sides of the Atlantic. The Dutch captured Elmina on the Gold Coast from the Portuguese in 1637 and attacked other forts as part of a concerted campaign to usurp the Portuguese positions on the world sea routes. We have already looked at their activities in the Indian Ocean region, so it is appropriate to consider the western half of the campaign.

The Dutch West India Company (*West Indische Compagnie*) was founded in 1621. It was financed, like its eastern counterpart, by the investments of shareholders, but its management board (*Heeren-19*) was effectively dominated by Calvinist refugees from the southern Netherlands, whose ideological stance was strongly anti-Catholic and, therefore, anti-Iberian. In 1630 the Dutch captured the Portuguese colony of Pernambuco, the main port for the prosperous sugar-growing region. They imported thousands of slaves from the West African slaving ports, which they took from the Portuguese. In 1644 the West India Company purchased nearly seven thousand slaves for export to the Americas. The Dutch administration of the sugar plantations did not last long, however. The staunchly Calvinist Dutch were eventually driven out in 1654 by the Catholic

Portuguese and Creole population, in spite of Dutch naval supremacy. In spite of their defeats in Brazil and their supposed exclusion from the Caribbean according to the terms of the Peace of Westphalia (1648), the efficient and ambitious maritime merchants of the Netherlands established themselves as major carriers of sugar and other produce between Europe, Africa and the New World.

British and French conquests and colonizations in the Americas in the seventeenth century brought their citizens into the growing sugar industry and slave trade as well. The first British colony at Jamestown, founded in 1607, was unable to grow sugar cane, nor was the relatively waterless island of Bermuda. When the island of Barbados was settled by the British in 1627, however, it proved an ideal place for sugar growing. Other British imperial possessions followed on the African coast as well, swelling the coffers of the slave traders and the colonial plantation owners and, through the taxes and duties levied, the British crown. Tariffs were set at rates that discouraged imports from the colonial possessions of other nations. By the middle of the seventeenth century the British sugar islands had overtaken Brazil as the main supplier to northern Europe. Production increased to meet the growth in demand throughout the seventeenth and eighteenth centuries. In Britain sugar consumption is estimated to have risen from four pounds to eighteen pounds per person between 1700 and 1800. Britain and France also established chartered trade companies, the English Royal African Company (1672) and the French Compagnie du Sénégal (1673), which were both private merchant ventures with varying levels of state support.

It should be emphasized, of course, that the sugar plantations did not furnish the only destinations for imported African slave labour. Diamond and gold mines in the interior of Brazil were major 'consumers' of slaves, as were the urban settlements that developed around them. The Brazilian cotton plantations which flourished in the eighteenth century were supplanted by those of the United States in the nineteenth century, but coffee growing increased rapidly and even overtook sugar as Brazil's main food export in the 1830s. Tobacco was the first agricultural crop to be produced mainly by slaves in North America, once again as a result of the unwillingness of sufficient immigrants to accept servile status and harsh working conditions. The rise of Britain's merchant and naval fleets in the late seventeenth century was accompanied by a sharp increase in the slave trade between Africa and the colonies of the south-eastern seaboard of North America. Rice and indigo were slave-produced crops in these areas, but towards the end of the eighteenth century the new cotton plantations of Alabama, Louisiana and Mississippi produced what was soon to become the heaviest demand for African slaves in the United States.

The Atlantic slave trade was not the only one in existence at this time. The slave trades of the Indian Ocean and Mediterranean regions go back well into antiquity, and in some areas they lasted into the twentieth century. Muslim and Christian slaves were available in many ports across the Mediterranean in the sixteenth and seventeenth centuries. All told the slave trade of the Old World must have accounted for many, many millions of slaves over the course of several millennia. What makes the Atlantic slave trade stand out is its rapid growth and its intensity. The bare statistical facts of the Atlantic slave trade are a stark testimony to the miseries which maritime expansion inflicted on the servile labour force. It is estimated that in the two centuries from *c.*1500 to 1700 around 500–600,000 African slaves were imported into Brazil, another 450,000 into the non-Iberian Caribbean and a further 400,000 to Spanish America. North America was a minor importer in this period, but between 1701 and the official termination of the Atlantic slave trade in 1808 a staggering six million persons were forcibly taken across the Atlantic by the slave ships.

They were purchased in relatively small quantities from disparate groups of African slave traders who had themselves obtained the slaves from a wide variety of sources, including kidnap victims, criminals and war captives. The slaves were gathered in holding areas, where they might spend months while a 'cargo' was assembled, and then embarked upon the infamous 'Middle Passage'. The journey across the Atlantic was far from comfortable even for a free sailor, but for the slaves, confined in ships which, despite the provision of ventilation and sleeping pallets, must always have been extremely unpleasant, it was a tortuous and often lethal journey. Dysentery and fever were the most common killers among the slaves, both in their holding pens and on board ship. Although the mortality rates do not seem very high at first glance, typically between 4 and 12 per cent, it is important to recognize that the majority of the slaves transported were young, healthy adult males (twice as many as females), whose ability to survive the journey was high.

The developments outlined above were part of what is often referred to as the triangular maritime trade system of the Atlantic. From Europe, especially Britain and France, manufactured goods, particularly textiles, were exported for sale in Africa. From Africa slaves were taken for sale in

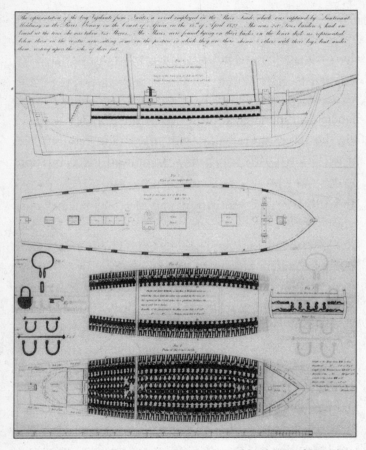

ABOVE: The French slave ship *Vigilante*, captured by the Royal Navy in the River Benin in 1822. There were 345 slaves on board. There is no doubting the priorities that underlay the most uncivilized and oppressive aspect of the expansion of seaborne commerce.

the Americas, and from the New World various commodities including rum (made from molasses), cacao (cocoa or chocolate), coffee and cotton, produced by the slave plantation system were shipped back to Europe and to parts of Africa and Asia. Ship builders, mariners, merchants and financiers all made great profits from these trades. Eventually, however, the advocates of free trade reduced the protectionist tariffs which had guaranteed the plantation owners their profits, making the system far less viable economically. There was a shift away from dependence upon servile labour in the early nineteenth century, when the governments of Britain and the United States were forced to bring the slave trade to an end. This was well before the onset of emancipation, however, which came in 1838 for the British possessions and 1848 for the French, but was not realized until 1865 in the United States. Brazil, Cuba and Puerto Rico were even slower to change their systems.

The global maritime trading expansion of the nineteenth and twentieth centuries has, of course, featured many other foodstuffs, produced by a wide range of servile, indentured, contracted and even landowning workers. Until the 1860s bananas, for example, were eaten in significant quantities only in the tropics, when they became the object of a considerable plantation-based production increase at the instigation of European and British financiers and traders. By the 1890s large companies had cleared away jungles, built railways, roads and even ports for the banana industry, which is now a major contributor to the economies of such countries as Brazil, Uganda, India and the Philippines. Tea drinking is taken for granted even more than the consumption of bananas by the citizens of the world's developed countries, yet its worldwide popularity is also a recent phenomenon. The Chinese and Japanese are known to have been avid tea drinkers since antiquity, but the European discovery of teas only really began in the sixteenth century. It was the Dutch East India Company that started the export of tea in substantial quantities to Europe in the seventeenth century. Production was mostly centred on China and the trade came through the ports of South-east Asia, until in the nineteenth century Indian, Javan and Ceylonese tea plantations were encouraged by the British East India Company. As tea has grown in popularity around the world, countries such as Argentina, Peru and Russia have become exporters, utilizing the global maritime trade networks to distribute their products.

Diseases and seaborne trade
Human beings have always had to contend with the pres-

ence of contagious and deadly diseases. As human civilization became more focused on sedentary agriculture, with its relatively limited dietary range, the variety of nutrients and vitamins available was reduced in comparison to that available to the prehistoric hunter-gatherers whose bodies were more readily able to resist disease. At the same time agricultural civilizations created conditions which encouraged new pathogens, some of them hosted by plants, insects and animals, others passing between human beings without any intermediate host. The process of building up immunities to these diseases was a very slow and, obviously, a very painful one. Different civilizations of the world developed their own particularly virulent diseases, smallpox evolving in South Asia and measles in China, for example. As many of these civilizations established maritime and overland trading links, they shared their diseases and, gradually, pooled their immunities, but the sudden, long-distance transmission by seafarers of pathogens to communities in areas previously untouched by them could cause immense suffering and loss of life.

An early example of an infectious disease spread by maritime communications networks is the plague which devastated Classical Athens in the fifth century BC, at the time of the Peloponnesian War (431–404 BC). It seems to have originated either in Persia or Egypt, and it spread along the well-established sea routes to Greece. It came to Athens in 430 BC and claimed, among its many victims, the Athenian statesman Pericles. The historian Thucydides, who caught the infection but survived, says that its first victims were among the people who lived in Piraeus, the port of Athens. He also points out that it was reported earlier to have struck on the island of Lemnos in the northern Aegean, which lay on the main trading route to the Hellespont and the Black Sea, and was controlled by the Athenians as part of their maritime empire. From these observations it is clear that the bacteria which caused the infection were being carried by ship. Athens was at war with the rival city-state of Sparta at the time and the Athenians had crowded into the urban area of Athens to shelter behind its impregnable walls. The overcrowded conditions seem to have encouraged the spread of the disease within the city. It is estimated that one third of the population died. While the death of Pericles robbed the Athenians of their leading statesman, it was probably the sudden, drastic decline in their population that had the greatest impact on their ability to maintain the naval power they relied upon to dominate the Greeks of the eastern Mediterranean. After a protracted struggle with the Spartans and their allies the

Athenians finally surrendered in 404 BC, relinquishing their overseas empire and destroying the defensive walls that had kept the enemy out for so long.

The plague of 430 BC seems to have been confined to the eastern Mediterranean, but an example on a greater scale is offered by the plagues which devastated the Roman Empire in the time of the Emperor Justinian (527–565). There had been plague outbreaks in the Roman Empire in the second and third centuries AD, but their identity is unclear. The plague outbreak of the 540s can be identified with reasonable certainty as bubonic. The contagion would have been carried by black rats and transmitted between them by fleas. Originating in either northern India or, possibly, north-east Africa, it seems to have been spread across the Roman Empire from Ethiopia and had reached as far as the British Isles by *c.*545. The extensive maritime trading links between the Indian Ocean and the Mediterranean region undoubtedly helped in the spread of this plague. The port cities of South Asia, the Persian Gulf, the Red Sea and the Mediterranean were, as we have already noted, highly cosmopolitan places. Their busy communities of merchants and other seafarers, travelling along the established sea routes, were unwittingly providing the means for infected black rats to move from one port to another. The bacteria which carry the plague infection, *Pasteurella pestis*, are not continuously present in the rat population, indeed they are as lethal to the rats as they are to humans. Modern research indicates that the rats probably acquired the disease in Africa, and began transmitting it to humans when they adapted to living in an urban environment around the start of the first millennium AD. The collection and (temporary) storage of foodstuffs and other organic materials in the warehouses of the flourishing trading ports provided an excellent environment for black rats. They moved around the Indian Ocean region more readily than they might have done across large land areas because they were able to climb up mooring ropes on to ships in search of food, which was being carried by sea in large quantities by this time. If the plague did start to cause problems in the Indian Ocean region some considerable time before it spread north, resistance and immunity may have begun to appear among the populations there, somewhat reducing its virulence. When it traversed the land barrier of Egypt into the Mediterranean, however, it encountered a population with no such resistance.

Ironically the maritime trade network which helped to spread the disease was one of its notable victims. The plague outbreaks precipitated substantial declines in population and consequent reductions in agricultural production and, above all, in urban wealth accumulation and expenditure. These factors tended to reduce the volume and frequency of maritime trade in those areas where the plagues were most serious. It could be said that plagues had a major depressive effect on the economy of the Indian Ocean, the Middle East and the Mediterranean, adding to the literal and spiritual sense of darkness caused by a catastrophic volcanic eruption in the 530s and the subsequent world-wide weather disruption and famines. Several further pandemics in the sixth and the first half of the seventh centuries were largely confined to the eastern Mediterranean, but in the second half of the seventh century there were more severe and widespread plague outbreaks which affected the Muslim and Christian worlds. Eventually the infection died out because it could not establish itself anywhere in a natural host population.

The arrival in Japan in the 520s of Buddhist missionaries from Korea, which we noted in the previous chapter, may have been the unheralded occasion of the introduction of smallpox to the Japanese islands. Further epidemics followed, as the Japanese became increasingly integrated into the maritime communities of the Far East, until the great smallpox epidemic of 735–7 which wiped out roughly one third of the population. This disaster sorely tested the faith of the Japanese people in its emerging Ritsuryo rulers. Emperor Shomu, a devout Buddhist, saw the sufferings as evidence of divine disapproval of his own inadequacies as a ruler. He decided, therefore, to heighten his own and his people's piety by living a more virtuous life and ensuring the construction of many shrines throughout the provinces of Japan. The problem the Japanese faced, however, was that their island locations and their relatively small population meant that increased maritime contacts brought increased risk of new epidemics. Bubonic plague reached Japan from China in the first decade of the ninth century and many epidemics of plague, mumps, measles and smallpox followed, until Japan eventually became integrated into the disease patterns of the East Asian mainland around the thirteenth century.

In the fourteenth century bubonic plague was once again on the move. It penetrated China with devastating effect in 1331 and was then carried along the caravan routes through central Asia. These routes were heavily used in the fourteenth century, partly as a result of the political linking together of vast territories by the Mongol conquests under Genghis Khan and his successors. The spread of this notorious pandemic, known in Europe as the 'Black Death', was once again assisted by maritime commerce. It spread westwards from central Asia in the 1340s, reaching the Crimea by 1346 and Constantinople by 1347. From these points it was carried swiftly across the maritime networks of the Mediterranean and beyond, reaching England and the Low Countries in 1348–9. It probably came to Scandinavia via the ports of England and Germany in the 1350s. The bacteria's invasion of a region via its seaports was quickly followed by penetration inland, again following the trade routes which connected the ports with their economic hinterlands. The few large areas of Europe known to have been spared the attacks of the Black Death are well inland, such as the southern Polish plains in central Europe and the Béarn region of southern France. Later outbreaks followed a similar pattern to those of the sixth and seventh centuries, recurring after a little over a decade. The effects of these plagues on population, agriculture, the commercial economy and political and social coherence could be devastating. In England, for example, the population in 1400 is estimated to have been only half that of 1300. Violent uprisings, such as the French Jacquerie of the 1350s, were partly caused by the dislocation of economic and social life produced by the Black Death.

The epidemiological research which finally identified

the bacteria that cause bubonic plague and highlighted the infectious relationships between fleas, rodents and humans, was prompted by another terrifying outbreak at the end of the nineteenth century. The cause in this instance seems to have been a Chinese military expedition to Yunnan province in the mid 1850s, where the plague had become endemic. Soldiers sent to the region to put down a serious revolt carried it back into central China, where it spread with relative slowness via overland communications networks until it reached the international trading ports of Hong Kong and Canton in 1894. From these places it was spread across the world via the global maritime trade routes. The infected humans and animals were carried at much greater speed and across far greater distances than had been possible for their medieval counterparts. By the early 1900s it had struck, in some cases with devastating effect, in Bombay, Sydney, San Francisco and Buenos Aires. The speed and size of the merchant vessels of the early twentieth century allowed the infection to cross the enormous distances of the Pacific, Indian and Atlantic Oceans before it killed off all the potential human and animal hosts available to it on any particular ship.

The infection of the New World

Exchanges of diseases within the main regions of the Old World had gradually led to a relatively stable situation by the end of the fourteenth century. The opening out of the maritime world at that time inaugurated a new phase in the biological history of world civilizations. The developing trade routes which stimulated economic growth and facilitated cultural exchange played a major part in the global spread of serious diseases. Epidemics of measles, smallpox and bubonic plague (or similar, uncertainly identified diseases) were quite commonplace throughout the history of the Old World. The opening up of maritime connections between the Old World and the New saw the introduction of several contagious and deadly diseases to the Americas. Columbus' famous voyage of 1492 paid host to a veritable pandemonium of infectious diseases which, while dangerous in their European setting, were catastrophically lethal once they were let loose on the populations of the New World. The Arawaks of the Caribbean Islands, and after them their mainland cousins, were assaulted by strains of smallpox, measles, influenza and typhus in quick succession.

Swine influenza may well have been the first major killer, affecting the newly arrived Spanish almost as much

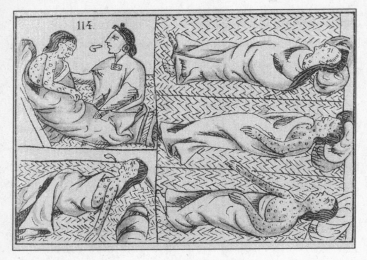

ABOVE: This graphic illustration comes from the Florentine codex, an account of the conquest of Tenochtitlán by an eyewitness. It shows the agonies of the victims of the smallpox epidemic introduced by Cortés in 1520. The Aztec source referred to the disease as 'the great rash'. It accounted for approximately one third of the total population.

as the natives. Smallpox was introduced into the Caribbean by the Spanish in 1518, where it reputedly left only a thousand survivors among the native population. Then it was taken to the mainland by Cortes' reinforcements in 1520 (see Illustration 16, above). The Aztecs, Mayas, Incas and other peoples swiftly succumbed to it in very large numbers because of their total lack of immunity, making the Spanish conquests much easier than they might otherwise have been, as we have seen. They were both slaughtered and demoralized by the disease which, it must be stressed, both they and their Spanish attackers readily interpreted as a manifestation of divine displeasure. Measles broke out a decade later, followed by typhus in 1546, which was a new experience for the Europeans as well, illustrating how easy the maritime links between the Americas and Europe made it for the two regions to 'share' in the spread of epidemics. Similarly the influenza epidemic of the 1550s struck down millions in Europe and the Americas, and it may even have reached as far as Japan.

The European maritime expansion of the fifteenth century undoubtedly also facilitated the spread of smallpox to sub-Saharan Africa. Nor was this the only seaborne exchange of diseases between Europe and other parts of the Old World. The origins of the syphilis epidemics that raged across Europe and Asia in the late fifteenth and early sixteenth centuries are disputed, but one view holds that it was the Portuguese plantation overseers and slave traders whose interactions with the native West African population transmitted existing yaws infections into the more temperate climates of the Mediterranean, where they mutated into syphilis. The subsequent importation of thousands of slaves, predominantly young females, into Iberia and other parts of Europe would have helped to spread the disease. The traditional alternative view is that syphilis was brought to Europe from the Americas by the soldiers and sailors on Columbus' first voyage to the Caribbean. The timing of the earliest recorded outbreak of the disease, in 1494, and its location, among the army of the French monarch Charles VIII in Naples, would seem to fit this hypothesis very well. The dispersal of this largely mercenary army after Charles' withdrawal would have encouraged a rapid spread of the disease. It was then carried out to India by Vasco da Gama's expedition of 1498 and from there spread via the maritime trade routes to China and Japan in the early years of the sixteenth century.

The royal licence to import African slaves to the Caribbean was granted by the Emperor Charles V, in 1518, partly in response to the need to replace the decimated indigenous population with Negroes who shared the same range of immunities to disease as their European masters. Several new pathogens crossed the Atlantic with the slave ships. The spread of malaria and yellow fever from the Old World to the New World in the sixteenth and seventeenth centuries is yet another example of the unexpected effects of global seafaring. Scholars have deduced that the mosquitoes which carried these infections were given an ideal form of transport in the large water casks that sailors depended upon to sustain them on the long voyages.

The flow of Negro slaves across the Atlantic to the Caribbean Islands and the American mainland gradually replaced the vulnerable native Americans with people who had already acquired a certain degree of resistance and immunity to the diseases that had virtually wiped out the indigenous population. When the slave trade slackened off and the relative health of people travelling between the continents improved, so did the population levels. The long-term result, however, was the reduction of the indigenous pre-Columbian population of the Americas to something like one twentieth of its original level.

Voyages of exploration such as those of Captain James Cook (1728–79) also transmitted diseases to the more isolated parts of the world, with what we can now call predictable results (see Map B, p. xii). It has been estimated that 90 per cent of the indigenous population of the Hawaiian Islands died from imported diseases in the eighteenth and nineteenth centuries. In Australia and Oceania and some of the remoter parts of the Americas the effects of the introduction of the rest of the world's illnesses are still being felt. The long-term result of increased maritime communication between the ports of Europe, Asia, America and other parts of the world was, however, a general stabilization of the patterns of infection so that, once the problems of poor sanitary arrangements had been overcome, populations were able to grow in spite of the presence of endemic disease. The story of the transoceanic exchange of diseases is far from over, however, as the spread of the AIDS virus from its apparent origin in Africa to the rest of the world all too vividly demonstrates.

VI

CONCLUSIONS

The technology of seafaring has come a long way from its prehistoric origins. Larger, faster, more dependable ships have been built to carry people and property along sea lanes that span the globe. The great oceans of the world no longer represent the ultimate challenge to humanity's genius for invention and daring, but they still act as the main highway of the modern world economy. A major theme of this book has been the development of extensive maritime networks that have linked civilizations together through trade, the projection of political power and the diffusion of ideologies and cultures.

A study of maritime networks dominated by some of the world's most celebrated seafaring societies has shown that there was a major historical development, beginning around 1500, when several European nations rapidly expanded their maritime networks. An important feature of this expansion was the way that it transcended long-established regional boundaries. Spanish, Portuguese, Dutch, French and English ships projected the political and economic power of these nations across the globe. The intensive exploitation of the new trade routes and territorial possessions brought great wealth and power to the Europeans, and other nations, and led ultimately to the creation of a world economic and political power network. These achievements can, of course, be viewed in a very positive light, but there are negative aspects to the stories of seafaring triumph, not least the oppressive and parasitical nature of the relationships established between some of the great maritime nations and other, less powerful peoples.

Why was it the relatively small nations of western Europe, rather than the vast states of Ming China, or the Ottoman, Safavid and Afghan Empires, that were able to use their seafaring skills to expand their economic and political networks? Technological developments cannot be taken as the decisive factor in the shift from co-operation to conflict and conquest. It might be true that western European firearms and naval vessels were superior to those of other peoples, but that does not mean that in a military clash the Europeans were bound to come out on top. Wider considerations of resources are very important. In projecting their power over such great distances they stretched their manpower resources to the limits. The decline in the influence of Portugal and the Netherlands in particular can be partly accounted for by population constraints, whereas the maritime expansions of Britain, France and later the United States were accompanied by substantial population increases.

Organizational advantages, including centralized governments keen to lessen their dependence on revenues drawn from internal taxation, chartered investment companies with quasi-governmental authority and well developed financial systems, can all be adduced to help explain European success. Nor should the unrelenting focus on commercial motivations and rewards be overlooked. Political divisions and rivalries in certain regions meant that often the opportunities existed for intervention by external maritime powers, and competition among the states of Europe certainly played a part in encouraging their overseas ambitions. The rivalries between Venice and Portugal, Spain and the Netherlands, England and France were at different times political, religious and commercial in emphasis, but they were unrelenting and their intensity grew as

they were acted out on an industrialized, global stage. The impressive growth of the United States and the modernization of Japan in the nineteenth and twentieth centuries increased that intensity still further. The world-wide maritime economy was, unfortunately, a prerequisite for the world wars.

There is also something to be said for the way that the maritime topography of Europe shaped the accomplishments of its most ambitious seafarers. From Norway to Iberia the westward-facing littorals presented an opportunity, or challenge, to master the open waters of the ocean and voyage into the regions beyond their home seas. Similar points might be made about the Indian Ocean, but there the combination of a pattern set by the prevailing winds and the powerful attraction of the territorial empires of Asia seems to have limited the horizons of its mariners more effectively. From the shores of the Americas also the

OPPOSITE: The people in the foreground of this unusual photograph from 1932 seem oblivious to the Finnish cargo ship *Penang*, which looms behind them at a dry dock in Millwall, South London. The picture encapsulates the way that seafaring's essential contribution to the development of modern civilization has been pushed to the background of most people's awareness. There is a sad echo of the destructive side of seafaring and civilization in this picture: in 1940 the *Penang* was torpedoed and sunk. There were no survivors.

vastness of the Atlantic and Pacific Oceans do not appear to have exerted sufficient attraction to draw the seafaring civilizations out into the great unknown.

We have noticed, very clearly in the cases of Islam and Christianity and also in the case of Buddhism, that the spread of proselytizing religions was greatly aided by maritime links. Seafaring merchants often seem to have been in the vanguard of the bearers of new ideas to distant places. When reflecting on some of the less noble topics that have been studied in this book, however, we cannot but notice that the sea has often provided a way of separating civilized people from many of the moral and religious constraints of their own societies, thereby freeing them to act on distant shores in ways that they would not have contemplated close to home. In religious terms it could be argued that the expansion of European maritime networks was often far too rapid to be kept pace with by the ideological counterpart of Christianity. While the conquered territories of the New World were nominally Christian from the outset, in reality its indigenous cultures retained their own religious identity and the European immigrants struggled to adapt their ideological frameworks to the new circumstances. In Asia and East Africa, in contrast, where Islam and Buddhism had long been spreading across the seafaring networks, the pace of change has been more reasonable in spite of the growth of Christianity.

The overseas production and maritime distribution of foodstuffs are surely a major example of the positive contribution that seafaring has made to the evolution of many civilizations. New sources of foods have been developed and new foods incorporated into the diets of many peoples. Often this has led to the creation of new social and economic structures, which, as we have seen in the case of sugar production, has not always been to the benefit of the societies caught up in such developments. The association between seafaring and slave trading is a topic that brings little credit to any of those involved.

As well as the deliberate movement of people, goods and ideas across the world's oceans we have seen that serious illnesses can also be transported to new regions with striking consequences. Nothing can be more starkly indicative of the potential for humanity's ingenuity to have unforeseen and devastating consequences than the spread of diseases by sea. Indeed, the eminent historian William McNeill has described the world as 'still reverberating to the shocks inaugurated by the new permeability of ocean barriers that resulted from the manifold movement of ships across the high seas after 1492'.[1]

The expanded global economy has also generated serious environmental problems. An unfortunate result of the modern world's relentless technological and industrial progress is the alarming amounts of hazardous, poisonous and even radioactive substances that are dumped into the seas from ships, sewage outfalls and polluted rivers.

There are clearly many adverse consequences that can be deduced from our study, but they should not be allowed to wholly overshadow positive perspectives on seafaring and civilization: for example, the spread of Christianity and other religions into new regions, and the advances in maritime technology that were at once both encouraged by and contributed to the growth of global networks. The long-term development of the modern economy, for all its inequalities and its potential for harm, can still be seen as a great step forward in the development of human civilization.

Culturally, too, the world has benefited from its mariners' endeavours. The rich heritage of Iberian culture that was spread by sailors, traders, settlers and missionaries flourished in many places and has produced an impressive legacy. Spanish is the third most widely spoken language in the world, the first or second language of people in places as far away from Spain as Chile and the Philippines. English has become even more widespread, as have many aspects of English culture, as can be said of the cultures of other European maritime nations. Such influences do, of course, work both ways. Any reader of this book will surely be able to think of aspects of his or her language, diet, dress, creative arts and everyday culture that have their origins overseas.

Whatever perspective we choose to view it from, the contribution of seafaring to the evolution of civilization has certainly been rich, varied and fascinating. Finally, we should reflect with genuine admiration on the way that, time and time again, the mariners of all the great seafaring civilizations have found the confidence to pit the resources and skills at their disposal against the challenge of the sea.

We began this book with a quotation and it is appropriate to end it with another, this time taken from a poem by H. W. Longfellow (1807–82), entitled, *The Secret of the Sea*:

'Wouldst thou' – so the helmsman answered –
  'Learn the secret of the sea?
Only those who brave its dangers
Comprehend its mystery!'

REFERENCES

Chapter I   **Navigation**
1   Byock, Jesse L., *Medieval Iceland: Society, Sagas and Power*, University of California Press, Berkeley, 1988, p. 1.

Chapter II   **Trade**
1   Petronius, *The Satyricon*, translated by Paul Dinnage, Panther Books, London, 1971, pp. 92–3.
2   McPherson, Kenneth, *The Indian Ocean. A History of People and the Sea*, Oxford University Press, Delhi, 1993, p. 55.
3   *The Life of the Admiral Christopher Columbus by his son Ferdinand*, translated by Benjamin Keen, Rutgers University Press, New Brunswick, 1959.

Chapter III   **Empires**

1   Rothermund, Dietmar, *An Economic History of India from pre-colonial times to 1991*, Routledge, London, 1993, p. 16.

Chapter IV   **Religions**

1   *The Letters and Instructions of Francis Xavier*, n. 15, translated by M. J. Costelloe SJ, Institute of Jesuit Sources, St Louis, 1992, p. 46.

Conclusions

1   McNeill, William H., *Plagues and Peoples*, Basil Blackwell, Oxford, 1977, p. 234.

FURTHER READING

The most accessible and reliable general guide to the history of the world is the fourth edition of *The Times Atlas of World History*, edited by Geoffrey Parker. The numerous annotated maps make it particularly useful. The concept of economic and political power networks is discussed in more sophisticated terms by Michael Mann in *The Sources of Social Power. Volume I: A history of power from the beginning to A.D. 1760.*

The developments discussed in chapter I are covered in Richard Woodman's *The History of the Ship. The comprehensive story of seafaring from the earliest times to the present day*, which concentrates on seafaring from *c.*1500 onwards. For earlier periods see Lionel Casson, *The Ancient Mariners. Seafarers and Sea Fighters of the Mediterranean in Ancient*

Times; Gillian Hutchinson, *Medieval Ships and Shipping* and the chapters by Seán McGrail, A. J. Parker and Sarah Arenson in E. E. Rice, *The Sea and History*.

For chapter II the study by Philip Curtin of *Cross-Cultural Trade in World History* gives a general outline and discusses theoretical concepts. I have found the works by Kenneth McPherson, *The Indian Ocean. A History of People and the Sea*; Amélie Kuhrt, *The Ancient Near East c. 3000–330 BC*; Peregrine Hordern and Nicholas Purcell, *The Corrupting Sea: a study of Mediterranean history* and Barry Cunliffe, *Facing the Ocean: the Atlantic and its Peoples 8000 BC to AD 1500* stimulating and informative. On China see Jacques Gernet, *A History of Chinese Civilization*.

For chapter III G. V. Scammell's *The World Encompassed: The first European Maritime Empires c. 800–1650* is an excellent starting point. See also Lionel Casson, Jacques Gernet, and Fernand Braudel, *The Mediterranean and the Mediterranean World in the Age of Philip II*; Carlo M. Cipolla, *Guns, Sails and Empires: Technological Innovation and the Early Phases of European Expansion 1400–1700*, Michael Wood, *Conquistadors* and Paul Butel, *The Atlantic*. Dietmar Rothermund, *An Economic History of India from pre-colonial times to 1991* is a good introduction to the British in India and Eric Hobsbawm's *The Age of Capital 1848–1875* discusses the wider issues of nineteenth-century economic growth and political developments.

The issues discussed in chapter IV are touched upon by many of the works already mentioned. For a fuller discussion of early Buddhism see Himanshu P. Ray, *The Winds of Change. Buddhism and the Maritime Links of Early South Asia,* Jacques Gernet on China and Conrad Totman's, *A History of Japan.* There are useful entries on missionaries in the *Biographical Dictionary of Christian Missions.* The Icelandic conversion is analysed by J. L. Byock, *Medieval Iceland: Society, Sagas and Power* and the spread of Christianity in general in *The Oxford Illustrated History of Christianity.* On the significance of Muslim seafarers and traders see Philip Curtin, Kenneth McPherson and the fascinating study by S. D. Goitein, *A Mediterranean Society. The Jewish Communities of the World as Portrayed in the Documents of the Cairo Geniza.* The main religious elements in the development of the United States are outlined in Philip Jenkins, *A History of the United States.*

The relationship between seafaring and the spread of particular foodstuffs in the Indian Ocean region is dealt with by Kenneth McPherson; see also Jacques Gernet on China. The study by Sidney Mintz, *Sweetness and Power: the place of sugar in modern history* is very informative, and the wider issues of the slave trade are discussed in *The Atlantic Slave Trade* by Herbert S. Klein. On diseases the fundamental work is William H. McNeill's *Plagues and Peoples,* which can be supplemented by W. F. Bynum and Roy Porter's *A Companion Encyclopedia of the History of Medicine.*

All the books mentioned above have their own bibliographies that can be used to find more detailed works on particular subjects.

BIBLIOGRAPHY

Anderson, Gerald H., ed., *Biographical Dictionary of Christian Missions* (Macmillan, New York, 1998)

Barraclough, Geoffrey, ed., *The Times Atlas of World History*, fourth edition, edited by Geoffrey Parker (Times Books, London, 1978 and 1993)

Braudel, Fernand, *The Mediterranean and the Mediterranean World in the Age of Philip II*. Translated by Siân Reynolds (William Collins, London, 1972)

Butel, Paul, *The Atlantic*. Translated by Iain Hamilton Grant (Routledge, London, 2000)

Bynum, W. F. and Porter, Roy, eds., *A Companion Encyclopedia of the History of Medicine* (Routledge, London, 1993)

Byock, Jesse L., *Medieval Iceland: Society, Sagas and Power*

(University of California Press, Berkeley, 1988)

Casson, Lionel, *The Ancient Mariners. Seafarers and Sea Fighters of the Mediterranean in Ancient Times* (Princeton University Press, Princeton, 1959 and 1991)

Cipolla, Carlo M., *Guns, Sails and Empires: Technological Innovation and the Early Phases of European Expansion 1400–1700* (Minerva Press, New York, 1965)

Cunliffe, Barry, *Facing the Ocean: the Atlantic and its Peoples 8000 BC to AD 1500* (Oxford University Press, Oxford, 2001)

Curtin, Philip D., *Cross-Cultural Trade in World History* (Cambridge University Press, Cambridge, 1984)

Dinnage, Paul, *The Satyricon* (Panther Books, London, 1971)

Gernet, Jacques, *A History of Chinese Civilization* (Cambridge University Press, Cambridge, 1982 and 1996)

Goitein, Shlomo Dov, *A Mediterranean Society. The Jewish Communities of the World as Portrayed in the Documents of the Cairo Geniza* (University of California Press, Berkeley, Los Angeles and London, 1967)

Hobsbawm, Eric J., *The Age of Capital 1848–1875* (Weidenfeld and Nicolson, London, 1975; Sphere Books, London, 1985)

Hordern, Peregrine and Purcell, Nicholas, *The Corrupting Sea: a study of Mediterranean history* (Blackwell Publishers, Oxford, 2000)

Hutchinson, Gillian, *Medieval Ships and Shipping* (Leicester University Press, London, 1994)

Jenkins, Philip, *A History of the United States* (Macmillan, London, 1997)

Klein, Herbert S., *The Atlantic Slave Trade* (Cambridge University Press, Cambridge, 1999)

Kuhrt, Amélie, *The Ancient Near East c. 3000–330 BC* (Routledge, London, 1995)

Mann, Michael, *The Sources of Social Power. Volume I: A history of power from the beginning to A.D. 1760* (Cambridge University Press, Cambridge, 1986)

McManners, John, ed., *The Oxford Illustrated History of Christianity* (Oxford University Press, Oxford, 1990)

McNeill, William H., *Plagues and Peoples* (Basil Blackwell, Oxford, 1977)

McPherson, Kenneth, *The Indian Ocean. A History of People and the Sea* (Oxford University Press, Delhi, 1993)

Mintz, Sidney W., *Sweetness and Power: the place of sugar in modern history* (Viking, New York, 1985)

Ray, Himanshu P., *The Winds of Change. Buddhism and the*

Maritime Links of Early South Asia (Oxford University Press, Delhi, 1994)

Rice, E. E., *The Sea and History* (Sutton, Stroud, 1996)

Rothermund, Dietmar, *An Economic History of India from pre-colonial times to 1991* (Routledge, London, 1988 and 1993)

Scammell, G. V., *The World Encompassed: The first European Maritime Empires c. 800–1650* (Methuen, London, 1981)

Totman, Conrad, *A History of Japan* (Blackwell Publishers, Oxford, 2000)

Wood, Michael, *Conquistadors* (BBC Worldwide, London, 2000)

Woodman, Richard, *The History of the Ship. The comprehensive story of seafaring from the earliest times to the present day* (Conway Maritime Press, London, 1997)

INDEX